THE GOD WHO BECOMES REDUNDANT

The God Who Becomes Redundant

DIARMUID Ó MURCHÚ MSC

THE MERCIER PRESS LTD
FOWLER WRIGHT BOOKS LTD

The Mercier Press Limited
4 Bridge Street, Cork
24 Lower Abbey Street, Dublin 1

Fowler Wright Books Limited
Burgess Street, Leominster, Herefordshire, England.

British Library Cataloguing in Publication Data
  Ó Murchú, Diarmuid
    The God who becomes redundant
    1. Religion and sociology
    I. Title
    306'.6   BL60

    ISBN 0-85342-754-2 (Mercier Press)
    ISBN 0-85244-041-3 (Fowler Wright Books)

Printed by Litho Press Co., Midleton, Co. Cork.

Contents

Dedication

To a confrère and friend who embarked on the quest
Amid turmoil and pain 'till he went to his rest.
A one-time professor, imparting a truth,
That fermented and ripened and then it struck root.

I leave to your memory this book that I write
And in it, I hope, is a glimpse and a sight
Of your profound wisdom that remains but a dream,
Come alive in recalling your person and name:

FR HUGH PATTON, MSC

Introduction

If I cannot bend the higher powers, I will stir up the lower depths.
— NORMAN O. BROWN

*And what rough beast, its hour come round at last,
slouches towards Bethlehem, to be born.* — W. B. YEATS

We cannot ask the question of God neutrally because, quite simply, we are not neutral about the answer. — JOHN SHEA

IN 1984, some thirteen million people within the EEC were unemployed, about 40% of whom had become redundant because of jobs being terminated. Right across the northern hemisphere redundancy and unemployment continue to create social chaos. Being out of work has become a way of life associated with dependency on State benefit, a feeling of uselessness, a deep sense of loss and feeling of inferiority, economically and socially. That unemployment can be an opportunity for new creative growth is a myth to which relatively few subscribe. A study in Britain in 1984 on 1,000 unemployed poeple showed that two-thirds of the group did nothing to give new orientation to their lives or new meaning to their existence. To have a job and accrue financial status therefrom are fundamental values of the capitalistic system of western society; these values are deeply ingrained and will persist for a long time yet. Meanwhile the unemployment figures rise and being without a job becomes progressively an accepted way of life. It is only one among many symptoms of the *paradigm shift* (Thomas Kuhn) affecting our world today.

Redundancy and unemployment are features of modern life. They permeate our entire value-system. We indiscriminately discard anything we no longer deem useful. Clothes tend to be cast aside in order to keep pace with each emerging fashion; repairing or recycling is unfashionable these days; the market provides a vast array of disposable goods. The castaway mentality has also made subtle and devious inroads on human relationships; rather than 'work through' a problem, it is more popular these days to 'opt out' or to 'cop out', and so we detect an increasing rate of marital infidelity and in general an increase in the fragmentation of human relationships. Even religion has become a disposable commodity, which we retain while it serves a useful purpose and discard when it no longer answers our needs.

This book is about religion and, consequently, about God, the one we consider to be the origin and the source of religion. It is not a theoretical work. Observation rather than speculation, practice rather than theory, experience rather than knowledge and intuition rather than rational thought, form the basis of our reflection. The book seeks to explore man's need for God, the origin and source of that need, the various expressions through which man has, and continues to, articulate that need and the intriguing process whereby we make God redundant or redeploy him, so that he will not unduly infringe on human affairs.

Much has already been written on this subject, but contrary to other books, the present work begins not with God but with man and this is precisely its uniqueness. It considers man rather than God to be the creator of religion. The great religious truths of our age, and, indeed, of every age, are primarily the creation of man and not of God. We human beings are responsible for the religion and religiosity, for the atheism and idolatry, for the agnosticism and bigotry and for the devotion and mysticism that have dominated human life for an estimated 70,000 years. Hinduism, the oldest formal religion known to us began to emerge about 2,000 BC and since then no less then ten surviving major religious systems have come into existence. To many people these religions contain definitive revelations of mysterious truths, totally unknown to previous generations and unchangeable for the rest of time. The phase of formal religion, a time-span of some 4,000 years, is a mere 6% of man's religious quest and the Christian phase, a mere 3%.

Before ever formal religious systems emerged human beings had searched, reflected, prayed and worshipped. *Homo Religiosus* has had a long history, with a tremendous variety of expression and versatility. It is generally assumed that our prehistoric ancestors were primitive, uncultured, savage and cannabalistic. These are fantastic claims whereby we judge and project onto former generations standards unacceptable to the modern mind. It is a logical procedure, but grossly misleading. As *anthropology* continues to probe and unfold the story of our human origins it becomes apparent that a reservoir and depth of meaning abides in our prehistoric existence. Our roots are very sacred and any attempt to touch that sacredness can only enhance the quality of contemporary life.

The present book delves into the past on the conviction that it is essential for the future we wish to create for ourselves on this earth. We live at a crucial moment in history; evolution seems to be on the brink of a major break-through and all around us we see the signs of a dying and decaying civilisation. Our mechanistic view of life, whereby we perceived each living unit – whether the human body or the nation – as a machine in its own right, that view of life which created the industrial revolution and massive technology of more recent times, is no longer a viable model for growth and progress. It seems no longer capable of serving the needs and aspirations of man, although still the dominant image and likely to remain so for some decades to come.

The twenty-first century will, in all probability, experience a momentum towards another view of life, namely, the *holistic* or *systems* view, which seeks to interpret all life-forms, including the universe as a whole, as a process of mutual interdependence, whereby individual parts do not act independently but in relationship with each other for the good of the whole, not on the basis of *cause and effect,* but rather on the principle of mutual interdependence. Already this new orientation, predicted by Teilhard de Chardin almost forty years ago, is beginning to take shape, interestingly and perhaps, ironically, the momentum is arising not from within Christianity but from the combined insights of biology, physics, anthropology, psychology and mysticism. The creative spirit of God is at work, where we might least expect him, but where, perhaps, he is always most effectively at work, *outside* or on the *fringes* of official religious systems:

> It will come about as the result of biochemical discoveries that will make it possible for large numbers of men and women to achieve a radical self-transcendence and a deeper understanding of the nature of things. And this revival of religion will be at the same time a revolution. From being an activity, mainly concerned with symbols, religion will be transformed into an activity concerned mainly with experience and intuition – an everyday mysticism underlying and giving significance to everyday rationality, everyday tasks and duties, everyday human relationships. (Words of Aldous Huxley, quoted in Anderson and Savery, p. 195).

In sharing this new vision – one of great hope for what it offers and one of great pain for what must be abandoned – I am particularly indebted to Fritjof Capra and Peter Russell (physicists), René Dubos and Lyall Watson (biologists), Carl Jung, Victor Frankl and Elizabeth Kubler-Ross (psychologists), Richard Leakey (anthropologist), Joachim Wach, Mircea Eliade and Ninian Smart (religious anthropologists), John Macquarrie and Walbert Buhlmann (theologians), Teilhard de Chardin, Mother Teresa of Calcutta and Roger Schutz of Taizé (prophets of the twentieth century). Most of these people I have never met, but their insights, vision and hope have deeply touched my life and I hope that this book, which owes so much to their inspiration, will earn them the further exposure their vision deserves.

The drop-off in religious practice in the west has been the subject of discussion and research in recent years. Formal religions are definitely losing credibility, yet, there is a wide interest in religious matters, often most powerfully articulated by those who try to prove that religion is totally irrelevant to human life. The present book was written with all these people in mind – those who have completely lost interest and those who live in the dread that what they have loved and cherished is no longer important. The book is intended for lay people, who are often confused and inadequately informed by the partial truth of one or other religious persuasion.

Religion is a global and historical phenomenon; all people irrespective of time and place have an inner need to believe. Without this 'faith' we simply atrophy, stagnate and die. Religion is also a human phenomenon, pertaining in an unique way to the human species. Consequently, its total truth can never be embodied or expressed within any one system, no matter how comprehensive that system may be. Religion has to do with life, life in all its richness and diversity; and not merely human life, but also the earth we inhabit, our globe as a living ecosystem. A hatred for the world and the things of the world, a theme which features to varying degrees in all the religious systems, is just one of the major misconceptions our new religious awareness seeks to address. The goodness of life at all levels, and the hurt (sin) we cause through infringing on that goodness, is the major challenge posed by the holistic vision outlined in this book. Religion too must respond to the challenge; otherwise it continues to decline, along that downward curve on which, in its formal sense, it is already clearly set.

Living in an era of change can be exciting, but also extremely disturbing. In a time of transition, death is taking place all around us and unless one has some familiarity with the process (the various stages being, *denial, anger, bargaining, depression and acceptance*), one experiences much pain and loneliness, features that are common in today's society. The transitional phase also exhibits a tendency towards entrenchment: proponents of the rising culture are perceived as dangerous and disturbing, while the guardians of orthodoxy 'dig their heels in' and refuse to budge. Such polarisation, which is basically a denial of the death process, generates distrust and confusion; it is particularly noticeable today in the official churches.

The present work, scanning as it does a vast range of human religious experiences, provides a framework in which the reader can explore his/her own religious feelings or lack of them and also analyses the evolving religious consciousness of our day. Above all else it is intended to reassure and hopefully to awaken a new zest for life in all potential readers.

For many in today's society, God has become redundant and, consequently, is no longer of much use to anybody. Yet, we never cease looking over our shoulders to see if he is still there. Like the hound of heaven he still haunts us and seemingly will continue doing so for time immemorial. Keeping him redundant serves no useful purpose. In the 1960s we tried killing him off and that didn't work (the 'Death of God' theology). We tried secularising him and we ended up with a bunch of idols which are driving us crazy (secularisation). The redundant God is still there awaiting re-employment – in our lives and in our world. The physicists are responding, so are the biologists and the psychologists; when will the churches and all of us affiliated to them take the plunge and encounter the God of a new tomorrow?

> I hold close the womb
> Where first life lies,
> And sigh a human sigh.
> And hope we learn to dance
> Before we learn to die. – RICHARD H. PRODEY

Bibliography

Anderson, M. S. & Savery, L. M., *Passages,* Harper & Row, 1973.
Kubler-Ross, Elizabeth, *On Death and Dying,* Macmillan Co., 1969.
Kuhn, Thomas, *The Structure of Scientific Revolutions,* University of Chicago Press, 1970.

1

Homo Religiosus: Origin and Destiny
(Anthropology)

Evolution is a value-laden process. — EDWARD E. SAMPSON

God is not the creator, but the mind of the universe.
— ERICH JANTSCH

The genuine universality of a religion is first attained where this religion. . . establishes positive relationship with the total development of the human race, which is to say with the universal history of mankind, especially with the general history of religion from its earliest stages. — ERNST BENZ.

SOME THIRTEEN billion years ago, a primordial explosion ocurred in the fiery, fluid mass of our universe, shooting its splinters as stars into the wide open spaces. Then, some four and a half billion years ago, our planet spun away as an independent satellite in the solar system. Three billion years ago, with the appearance of the first algae, 'life' emerged on earth. Fish appeared four hundred million years ago, and two hundred million years later, the first mammals.

Human Evolution

Man's appearance on earth is a relatively recent event. A crude form of human life, about which we know relatively little, seems to have existed about fourteen million years ago. Our first trace of what we may consider a genuine human species is that of *Homo Habalis,* dated at some two million years ago. To this group we attribute the discovery of fire, a significant event in the rise of human civilisation. Over the past two million years, humanity has evolved through a

Evolutionary Time Scale

Thousand Years Ago	Time Period*	Cultural Epoch†	Human Life Form
14,000	Pliocene		Ramapithecus
3,000			Australopithecus (Dart, 1925)
2,000	Lower Pleistocene		Homo Habalis (Leakey, Tobias & Napier, 1964)
1,000			
700			
500	Middle Pleistocene		Homo Erectus (Dubois, 1892)
		Lower Paleolithic	
200			Homo Sapiens Steinheimensis
100		Middle Paleolithic	
60–50	Upper Pleistocene		Homo Sapiens Neanderthalensis
40			Homo Sapiens Sapiens (Linnaeus, 1758)
		Upper Paleolithic	
13			Modern Man
12			
11	Holocene	Neolithic	
10			
9		Mesolithic	
8			
7		Copper Age	
6			
5		Bronze Age	
4			
3		Iron Age	
2 AD, 1			

* *Time Period:* Determined by glaciation change and alteration.
† *Cultural Epoch:* Initially determined by man's use of stone tools.

series of significant stages (outlined on page 14), with the features and characteristics of contemporary man already well established some 40,000 years ago.

More important than the different evolutionary stages are the cultural developments taking place over the various epochs. The discovery of fire (c. 600,000 years ago) enabled human beings to cook their own meat, fend off the cold of winter and drive away with blazing logs the great carnivores that posed a threat to safety and survival. With the discovery of fire came the initial awareness that humans were destined to be masters of the universe.

Next came the use of tools, hunting skills and plant-gathering. Our ancestors began to socialise and enjoy companionship for its own sake; by 150,000 BC cave-dwelling was quite common. At a non-verbal level, our primitive ancestors began to communicate quite effectively, and by 100,000 BC, humans had acquired the ability to speak.

Story-telling around the glowing fire provided the occasion and opportunity for man's initial experience of God and religion. Through the medium of the story, the meaning of life, the power behind the universe, the origin of all that existed, and many other topics were explored and explained. At this juncture (c. 70,000 years ago) *Homo Religiosus* enters the scene.

The Rise of Homo Religiosus

Robert Bellah outlines five developmental stages in the evolution of religion:

1. *Primitive Religion,* consisting largely of ritualistic behaviour, acting out in symbolic fashion primitive urges and dreams, a process which slowly unfolded over a time-span of some 50,000 years. According to Bellah, a close connection between the worlds of myth and reality characterised this phase and religious ritual is varied and spontaneous as local needs dictate. Ritual tends to take place within the clan or tribal context. Occasionally, rites or customs were transmitted from one group to another, but not with definite roles nor with specific structure and content.

Bellah gives scant attention to the *pre-ritualistic* phase, which is of paramount importance for understanding the origins of religion. By pre-ritualistic, I mean that period of time when religious belief and value were being articulated and integrated in an implicit rather

Significant Developments in Human Culture

Date, BC	Significant Event
2,000,000	Use of crude tools
600,000	Controlled use of fire
c. 200,000	First traces of conceptual thought
150,000	Human beings dwelt in caves
100,000 –50,000	Progressive development of articulate speech and script
60,000	Burials were quite extensive
50,000	Basketry, netting and 'hide' products
30,000	Primitive art begins to flourish
25,000	Chipped-stone tools and 'blades'
20,000	Flute music
17,000	Earliest forms of clothing
15,000	First houses
10,000	Pottery and domestication of the dog
8,000	Food production (mainly from wheat and barley)
7,000	Domestication of the ox; first altars
5,000	Script-writing well developed
4,350	Domestication of the horse; first villages
3,600	Temples
3,500	Use of the wheel; metal-smelting
2,600	Sea-going ships
1,200	Iron technology

than an explicit fashion. Initially, this took place through story-telling, even when there was no deliberate religious intent and no explicit religious ideas. In these primitive narratives, man acquired a new sense of feeling at home in the world, named the seasons and the elements of nature, grappled with the surrounding sense of mystery, which at times was awesome and attractive, but usually frightening and threatening. The cycle of night and day, seasonal changes, weather fluctuations, sexual reproduction, death and life, became dominant themes in primitive story-telling. The stories became powerful means of conveying meaning and understanding;

they became the myths out of which religion was born (more on this in chapter 2).

The story-telling phase of primitive religion can be safely dated to 70,000 BC, and lasted for anything up to 20,000 years. By 50,000 BC we have concrete evidence for *religious ritual,* expressed primarily in burial customs. The dead were frequently smeared with red ochre, a ritual substitute for blood, confirming a belief in an afterlife. Corpses were adorned with shells, pendants, necklace and, sometimes food. These customs clearly indicate that our primitive ancestors felt they were in contact with their dead who could influence worldly fortune for better or for worse.

Some anthropologists attribute religious significance to ancient animal bone deposits, dating back to about 300,000 BC. Our evidence for this claim is speculative rather than substantive and since religious awareness demands a certain level of consciousness (according to Eliade, *A History of Religious Ideas*, p. 5) it is difficult to envisage an explicit religious motif before 150,000 BC.

However, animal bone deposits have another important significance. They point to primitive man's closeness to nature, his deep respect for all life forms and for the animal kingdom in particular. Hunting, therefore, became yet another important medium for the expression of spiritual values and religious customs. Story-telling and hunting were closely related, the latter often providing material and motivation for the former. As our ancestors continued to articulate their religious beliefs, the cultural importance of animals (and the hunt) did not wane, as is often assumed; quite the contrary, in fact!

And this brings us to what many anthropologists consider to be a pivotal point in the growth of prehistoric religion, namely the development of art, commencing about 35,000 BC. Prehistoric art is almost exclusively religious, rich and diverse in symbolic expression, focusing largely on animals (especially, stags and ibexes) and animal forms, with the following dominant motifs: life after death, fertility and the hunt. Describing the religious import of primitive art, Pérez-Esclarín writes:

> Art was born in the bosom of religion. Primitive art was vitalistic, sensual, organic, fraught with religious symbolism. It boldly sought to transcend humanity's earthly experiences of a reality that seemed quite hostile. The paintings on the walls of pre-historic cave-dwellings show us human

Chronological Chart Showing the Emergence of Major Religious Systems

BC c. 2000	HINDUISM	
c. 1500	SHINTO (primitive form)	
c. 1200	JUDAISM	Abraham/Moses
	ZOROASTRIANISM	Zoroaster (660-583)
	TAOISM	Lao Tzu (604-504)
	CONFUCIANISM	Kung Fu-Tse (551-479)
	BUDDHISM	Gotama Buddha (563-483)
AD	CHRISTIANITY	Jesus (4 BC–AD 33[?])
600	ISLAM	Muhammad (570-632)
1500	SIKISM	Nanak (1469-1539)

beings struggling for life and vying with supra-terrestrial forces that control it. One can readily detect a sense of the sacred and the numinous in the carefully arranged monoliths that make up the awesome megalithic structure of a primitive age.

Bellah's 'primitive religion' covers a time-span of some 50,000 years (up to 20,000 BC approximately). During this time *Homo Religiosus* progressed from an implicit awareness of religion through a wide variety of religious expression. The implicit awareness itself seems to have been innately unfolding over thousands of years necessitating a certain internal and external human development for adequate and appropriate expression. We will return to this topic in chapter 3.

2.   *Archaic Religion,* the characteristic feature of which is the emergence of *cult,* based on a religious system of gods, priests, worship, sacrifice (in some sense), divine and priestly kingship. Bellah's second category, which may be roughly dated from 20,000 to 2,000 BC, describes that stage of religious consciousness wherein human beings begin to speculate about the gods, their presence in the universe and their powers of influence for both good and evil. Therefore, worship and sacrifice became the necessary modes of communication to beseech and pacify the divine rulers.

In religious practice, a great deal of variety and spontaneity prevailed. However, as the religious consciousness deepened, a tendency to structure and organise religious practice began to emerge. Of particular significance during this epoch is the creation of 'intermediaries' between the people and God whether shamans, kings, seers and priests. For what seems to be the first time in human history, religious status and class differentiation based on this status, emerged. According to Bellah, this social differentiation would have led to inter-group rivalry and struggle, often considered to be warfare between rival deities:

> The ensuing breakdown of internal order led to messianic expectations of the coming of a saviour-king in such distinct areas as Egypt on the one hand and Chou-period China, on the other. (Bellah, pp. 31-32).

The birth of formal religion was immanent!

3. *Historic Religion,* an epoch covering some three and a half thousand years, during which ten surviving major religious systems emerged (cf. page 18). Formal religion comprises a remarkably small proportion of the human religious story (about 6%) and is practically unnoticeable in the spectrum of human evolution. That it took religion so long to become formalised is perfectly understandable against an evolutionary and anthropological background; that it *should* have become formalised is not easy to understand; that it should remain formalised (rather than change and adapt) makes little historical or anthropological sense.

The Summerians (in the third millenium BC) seem to have been the first to develop a formal religious cult, with a wide variety but, nonetheless, standarised format of ritual and worship and an accompanying body of myth and literature. About this time, too, an extensive upsurge of religious belief took place in many parts of the then known world, especially in Egypt, India, the Near East, Greece and right along the Mediterranean. About 2,000 BC, Hinduism emerged as the first major religious system.

Two main factors mark the birth of formal religion:

(i). *A transformation in human consciousness:* Influenced by some new evolutionary impact, human beings, over a wide geographical area, became aware of themselves as creative and responsible people in the world. A universal desire to comprehend the fundamental structure of reality, and, through 'salvation', participate actively in it, seemed to prevail (Bellah, pp. 33-34). J. G. Bennet (p. 329) claims that the new consciousness marks a revolt against the unpredictability of the Gods:

> ... men had grown sick of their dependence upon divine rulers and priests claiming sole access to the supernatural world. The great religions of the world appeared and developed, in nearly every case, in a proletariate avid for the assurance of its own significance that religion alone could offer.

According to this claim, formal religion was created not to give God more importance in human life, but precisely for the opposite reason: to allow human beings to take more responsibility for their own destiny, by assigning the gods to a 'controlled', institutional structure. Consequently, formal religion may be considered to be the supreme form of idolatry, a charge frequently made by atheists and other conscientious objectors.

(ii). *A new perception of divine influence:* Man's perceived relationship with the gods changed quite radically with the acquisition of the new self-consciousness. No longer was divinity perceived or understood as an impersonal power or as a diversity of deities, ever interfering in human and earthly affairs. God now came to be regarded as somehow human and personal and capable of being influenced (even controlled) by human ingenuity. This tendency, known as *anthropomorphism,* first became apparent in transferring the divine attributes from the totem to the king. Over a period of time, the myths, which formerly sought to influence or petition a deity through the medium of tribal liturgy, now became legends of royal supernatural power and control, initially noted in Egyptian, Persian and Greek literature.

The personalisation of the god/gods does not have a definite pattern or progression in the major religions. Even today most of the Eastern religions have an inferior understanding of man and tend to perceive God in a vague and ill-defined mode of existence, while Marxism (which some would not consider religious at all) goes to another extreme, in perceiving man as a production-agent, and, therefore, a god-unto-himself, albeit a false one!

According to Bellah, the historic stage also marks the development of a four-class system; a political, military elite; a cultural, religious elite; a rural, lower-class group (peasantry) and an urban lower-status group (merchants and artisans). From this new class structure emerged some religious-based conflicts which today sound almost legendary: the Israelite prophet and king; the Islamic ulama and sultan; Christian pope and emperor; Confucian scholar-official and his ruler. Thus religion became an integral factor of both rebellion and reform in every human culture.

4. *Early Modern Religion:* Bellah considers the Protestant Reformation (which, he claims, has parallels in the other great religions) to be the apex and 'the most successfully institutionalised' movement, marking the transition from the historic to the early modern stage. Religious symbolism in this era is focused on the direct relationship between the individual and transcendent reality. Thus, the emphasis on personal faith and the salvation of one's individual soul, became supreme values. Bellah goes on to suggest that social systems with a built-in tendency to change in the direction of greater value-realisation were the outcome of this new emphasis.

There may be some truth in this observation vis-a-vis the Protestant churches, but for the Catholic Church, and apparently for the other major religous systems, it was a time of unhealthy, introverted, personal salvation, devoid of social conscience, prophetic witness and a sense of universal salvation which every religious system upholds. Because of this strong inward-looking attitude, reinforced by a close institutional set of perceptions, the nineteenth century became a period of strong and justifiable reaction to all forms of formal religion. In some cases, albeit a few, the reaction eventually led to renewal of the type experienced in the Catholic Church in the 1960s in the wake of the Second Vatican Council.

5. *Modern Religion:* For Bellah, the contemporary religious scene is one of shifting sands. The traditional, metaphysical world-view has broken down and the symbols used in former times to interpret the world metaphysically no longer function symbolically. Consequently, increasing numbers no longer look to formal religion for an ultimate understanding of life. Arising from the disillusionment with official religion is, on the one hand, a tendency to personalise the faith in an exclusively, individualistic manner, and, on the other, a tendency to locate one's search for meaning in secular, non-religious pursuits. On the part of the churches, Bellah notes a fluctuation from rigidities of the past to more liberal and tolerant positions, finally veering towards an 'orthodox' stance. The collapse of the old, institutional model has led to widespread disillusionment and confusion, but may in time, says Bellah, be viewed as one offering unprecedented opportunities for growth and innovation.

Religion Among Tribal Peoples Today

Complementing the anthropological evidence are a number of theories on the origins of religion. Towards the end of the nineteenth century, scholars began to study the religions of tribal peoples in today's society, especially Australian aborigines and North American Indians, in the hope of finding among them clues for the interpretation of religious behaviour in the ancient world. This approach is based on a number of unsatisfactory assumptions, not least among them being the belief that surviving primitive religions resemble those of prehistoric man.

Primitive man today is at a very different evolutionary point from his prehistoric counterpart. Contemporary tribal ritual and behaviour may seem ancient and out of touch with what is generally considered to be normative in our society; nonetheless these are expressions of life in the contemporary world and not in the ancient one. Their apparent archaicness may be due to resistance to the threat of outside influences or simply due to the closely-knit nature of the tribe. Behind the ritual performance, however primitive it may seem, is a group of people living in the twentieth century who, willy nilly, embody in themselves, in however small a way, the mindset, culture and mythology of our day. It would be naïve, and indeed, insensitive to evolutionary growth, to take tribal behaviours as prescriptive for the lifestyle of our primitive ancestors. However, taken in conjunction with the anthropological evidence outlined in the present work, current practice among tribal peoples provide some useful guidelines.

1. *Prehistoric man thought in pre-logical terms* (i.e. he could not recognise cause and effect) and consequently his perception of reality was archaic and inferior. One of the leading proponents of this theory, Lucien Levy-Bruhl (1857-1939), eventually retracted this proposition under the pressure of accumulating evidence to the contrary. Man's use of primitive tools, along with his hunting skills, clearly demonstrated the ability to comprehend cause and effect. That aside, the theory presupposes that logical thought is the norm for mature personhood, a conviction which is much debated today. There is good reason to believe that humanity, at some future point in its evolution, will develop a higher form of thinking based more on intuition than on logic. This does not mean that logical thought is inferior to the intuitive form. It simply means that thought can

also evolve in the course of history, with a different quality, appropriate for different times.

2. *Primitive man acted mainly out of instinct:* Wilhelm Koppers vehemantly challenges this theory. Drawing on a wide variety of ethnological evidence (some of which is quite dated) Koppers argues that primitive man, contrary to popular opinion, was quite domesticated, hunted and killed only for his own survival, had quite a developed sense of right and wrong and lived with his fellow humans in relative peace and harmony. This is not to say that cannibalism did not exist, but it seems to have been more a feature of '. . . agrarian, matriarchal forms of society in which the blood is regarded as the seat of the soul and as a peculiarly effective means of promoting fertility' (Koppers p. 6).

3. *Magic precedes religion:* This theory, mainly propounded by the late James G. Frazer, is outlined in his famous thirteen volume, *The Golden Bough.* Primitive people did not expect magic to do anything and everything. They use magic when their ordinary powers fail them in manipulating and controlling aspects of life which frighten and frustrate them. Magic is essentially practical and consists in fulfilling prescribed ritual acts, using spells and special formulae. Whereas magic seeks to control or manipulate the environment, religion consists primarily in submission to, trust in and adoration of, the object of attention.

With our highly developed understanding of religion today it is easy to distinguish it from magic. Such a distinction would be meaningless for primitive man. It is quite conceivable that our ancient ancestors tried to manipulate a frightening and alien universe through ritualistic formulae which today we would call magic. In contemporary primitive societies, magic often implies a rejection of, or reaction to, certain religious formulae and practices; in other words, it presupposes the existence of at least religious ideas. This, too, must have been true in prehistoric times; an effort to control superhuman forces implies some knowledge of these forces and recognises to some degree their power to influence man. Therefore, on no account can we claim that magic precedes religion; undoubtedly, something akin to magic frequently interrupted man's religious development at the various stages of his evolution.

4. *Primitive man worshipped one rather than many gods:* In a

scholarly work of some 1100 pages, Wilhelm Schmidt went to great pains to establish that our primitive ancestors believed in *one* rather than *many* gods; that this belief in monotheism originated and continued to be sustained by logical and rational thought; and that, therefore, anything other than belief in one god is alien to man's true nature.

There is little anthropological evidence to substantiate this position. Prehistoric belief did not concern itself with one or many Gods. Initially, it seems, God was perceived as a benevolent, universal power. Only about the third millenium BC did the idea of a personal god come to the fore in human thought; even then, monotheism did not dominate.

The ongoing debate on monotheism viv-a-vis polytheism is essentially an intellectual, philosophical one. In the experience of godliness (the subject matter of religious anthropology) the presence of God tends to be felt in an awesome but personal way, without God necessarily being perceived as a single person. Indeed, this creative tension between the one and the many, forms the basis for some of the most profound and complex dogmas (e.g. the Trinity in Christianity) in all the major religions in the world. Anthropologically, at least, the debate on whether god is one or many, is still an open question.

Other explanations for the origin of religion merit brief mention.

(a) In 1900, R. R. Marett coined the term, *Mana,* to explain belief in a type of impersonal power which our prehistoric ancestors sensed in the world and perceived to be favourably disposed to human welfare. According to Ninian Smart (p. 47), 'Mana is somewhat analogous to the idea an ignorant person has of electricity – powerful and unseen, capable of doing much for his benefit, yet capable too of destroying him.'

This explanation is based on the assumption, frequently and erroneously made, that our prehistoric ancestors could only perceive spiritual reality in a crude and primitive way. Increasingly, anthropologists acknowledge that the prehistoric mind may have had an intuitive and imaginative quality, connecting humans with basic truths of life which the rational and scientific mind of the twentieth century can only grasp in a fleeting and superficial way.

For our ancestors, the mysterious power called *Mana,* may well have been their keen sense of the *mysterium tremendum,* experienced through their close bond with nature, its cycles, elements and life-giving support. In the concept of *Mana* we are very likely naming not some magical, fantasised power, but the creative power of godliness and goodness within creation itself. At this level, prehistoric belief has striking similarities with the creation-based mysticism which forms an integral part of all the major religious systems known to us today.

(b) In 1871, E. B. Tylor propounded the theory of *Animism* as the origin of religion. According to this explanation, our primitive ancestors would have attributed the movement of water, the energy in fire and the power in wind to a 'soul' which inhabited these objects. Therefore, natural phenomena, which are presumed to contain a personalised spirit with hidden powers, became targets of fear, awe and admiration. In Tylor's view, religion originated in a great misunderstanding, based on ignorance and a low level of perceptual comprehension.

Once again, the theory downgrades prehistoric behaviour on the assumption that the contemporary, developed mind is normative for human understanding. From an anthropological viewpoint, it seems perfectly reasonable to suggest that our ancestors initially experienced the sacred through the medium of nature. Furthermore, their spontaneous response, which today we would call, 'worshipping false gods' was perfectly consistent with their lifestyle and environment. In all probability, these people were expressing a profundity of spiritual awareness far in excess of that embodied in the accepted modes of contemporary spirituality.

(c) *Totemism* is rooted in the primitive belief that members of a clan or tribe are united by kingship to some animal or plant from which they are descended. The totem is considered to be a sacred being, benevolent and helpful to humans. Ritually, the clan celebrates its common unity and allegiance in ceremonially consuming the blood of the totem animal. In this way religion serves both a social and spiritual function.

Totemism is best understood not as a possible origin for religion, but rather as a stage or phase in the development of religious consciousness. During this phase, which exhibits many features of Bellah's *Archaic Religion*, the social and ritualistic dimensions are quite highly developed and serve as a poignant reminder of a basic human need we all share, to express our religious beliefs in a social and ritualistic context appropriate to our needs and aspirations.

(d) *Shamanism:* in prehistoric times, the *shaman* was a type of specialist in religious matters, endowed with unique spiritual powers for the sake of the people and capable of absorbing in himself and communicating to others a special mode of sustaining and healing power.

In a major work on this topic, Mircea Eliade describes the shaman as an archetypal figure embodying in his person and lifestyle the deepest hopes and aspirations of the people among whom he lived. He is not a personification of a crude, primordial religious awareness. Rather, he is the product of a highly developed spiritual consciousness. In today's world, the monk (or religious) may be considered to be the contemporary counterpart.

Mana, Animism, Totemism, Shamanism are merely manifestations, particular historical expressions, of a rich and complex phenomenon which *Homo Religiosus* has been articulating for over 70,000 years. Our human, religious heritage is an integral part of our evolutionary growth and is deeply ingrained in our human fibre. We need to acknowledge this complexity if we are to reach an appropriate understanding of ourselves as creatures of God and of our world as the arena where God and man act out the drama of life and existence. Bergounioux and Goetz (quoted in Washburn, p. 116) seem to captivate this all-encompassing reality when they write:

> Thus we arrive at the great cosmic rituals, where we find sacrifice and mystery, animism and magic, totems and gods. . . but always the transcending God himself is subjected to the material, biological conditions of existence, and life itself is divinified as eternally cyclical and creative: God and the universe blend into a monist unit, sacrificing neither the reality of God outside the world, nor the reality of the world outside of God.

Towards an anthropology of Religion

It is impossible in the course of one chapter, or even in one book, to do justice to what anthropology has to offer for an exploration of the origin and growth of religion. The time-span is enormous, impinging influences are numerous, ritual and cultic expressions are extremely diverse, gaps in our knowledge (as in all branches of anthropology) are many; thorough research has scarcely begun.

Can we afford to wait until we have that type of concrete scientific evidence to satisfy contemporary scholarship? Doesn't all science emerge from initial gropings, intuitive insights, not a few errors, but yet an underlying current of compelling truth? How can one hope to analyse the religious phenomenon in any depth without first observing its emergence within the course of human evolution? In the absense of an anthropological perspective are we not in danger of obtaining a merely partial perception of truth, from which stance we can so easily create the ideological bias whereby genuine religion can easily become a form of idolatry?

Religion is a global phenomenon, transcending all creed and culture and deeply rooted in the primordial essence of human nature, individually and collectively. Anthropology leaves us in no doubt about that fact and further anthropological research will confirm rather than undermine that observation. Despite the limitations of concrete, factual data, the progressive evolutionary unfolding of the religious sentiment cannot be doubted; an underlying current, what we call the universal, human tendency to transcend, cannot be ignored; the massive array of religious expression (in cult, ritual, etc.) must be viewed much more critically, but not with the scientific scepticism of our age which is fundamentally alien to the spirit of our prehistoric origins.

The unfolding of the human *spirit,* rather than the human *fact,* is the focus of the anthropology of religion. The tools of research for this endeavour belong to the heart rather than the head: a passionate, patient, intuitive longing for the truth of what mankind has been, is and continually strives to become in the unfolding of the human story. The long and tedious hours spent in matching pieces of ancient skulls or analysing bone-deposits of prehistoric tombs, in dark and dreary cells, in frequently appalling working conditions, is a touching reminder of how far man is prepared to go to discover his origins. Anthropology is a vocation, a sacred mystical search, not an analytic, quantitative pursuit, but an exploration of inner space. At the end of the day its not the raw evidence that matters, but rather 'the dream come true', the discovery that seems to go on forever. We now follow that journey by studying the mythology of our ancestors, that powerful body of story, gesture and literature that gives expression to the deepest longings of our human religious heritage.

Bibliography

Anderson, R. T., *Anthropology: A Perspective on Man,* California: Wadsworth publishing Co., 1972.

Bellah, Robert, *Beyond Belief,* London: Harper & Row, 1970.

Bennet, J. G., *The Dramatic Universe,* Hodder & Stoughton, 1966.

Bergounioux, F. M. & Goetz, J., *Prehistoric and Primitive Religions,* Burns & Oates, 1965.

Collins, Desmond, *The Human Revolution: From Ape to Artist,* Oxford: Phaidon, 1976.

Eliade, Mircea, *A History of Religious Ideas,* Vol., 1: *From the Stone Age to the Eleusinian Mysteries,* University of Chicago Press, 1978.

——, *Shamanism: Archaic Techniques of Ecstasy,* Pantheon Books, 1964.

Frazer, James G., *The Golden Bough,* Macmillan & Co., 1967 (abridged edition).

Gribben, John, *Genesis,* London: Dent, 1981.

Koppers, Wilhelm, *Primitive Man and his World Picture,* Sheed and Ward, 1952.

Leakey, Richard, E., *The Making of Mankind,* New York: E. P. Dutton, 1981.

Levy-Bruhl, L., *The 'Soul' of the Primitive,* Allen & Unwin, 1965 (first published, 1928). His modified position of later years is outlined in his posthumous *Les Carnets du Lucien Levy-Bruhl* (published in English as *The Notebooks on Primitive Mentality,* Oxford: Blackwell, 1975).

Marett, R. R. *Threshold of Religion,* Methuen, 1914.

McKern, Sharon & Thomas, *Tracking Fossil Man: An Adventure in Evolution,* London: Wayland, 1972.

Péréz-Esclarín, Antonio, *Atheism And Liberation,* London, SCM Press, 1980.

Schmidt, Wilhelm, *The Origin and Growth of Religion,* Methuen, 1931.

Smart, Ninian, *The Religious Experience of Mankind,* Charles Scribner & Sons, 1969.

Tylor, E. B. *Primitive Culture,* London: Murray, 1871.

Washburn, S. L. (Ed), *Social Life of Early Man,* Methuen, 1962.

2

How the Religious Story Began to Unfold
(Mythology)

In the real world it is more important that a proposition be interesting than that it be true. The importance of truth is that it adds to interest. – A. N. WHITEHEAD

Telling stories is functionally equivalent to belief in God.

– SAM KEEN

Symbolism is not the apprehension of another world of archetypes, but the transfiguration of this world; and the transfiguration of this world is its reunification. – NORMAN O. BROWN

WITH THE DISCOVERY of fire (6–500,000 years ago) man's social life advanced significantly. A tendency to gather around the fire to share heat and food became the occasion too for primitive socialisation and recreation. It has been suggested that *Homo Erectus* (perhaps as far back as 200,000 years ago) developed the skill of story-telling around the glowing fire. Our suggested dates for the origin of articulate speech (*c.* 150,000 years ago) allow us to postulate that prelanguage was sufficiently developed by 200,000 BC to facilitate an archaic form of story-telling, which, of course, continued to develop over thousands of years. In these primitive tales we have the beginning of mythology, culture and ultimately, civilisation itself.

The Meaning of Myth

No concept evokes more interest today among social scientists than that of *myth* and *mythology*. For the average person the words connote a legendary tale concerning some ancient custom or practice, largely, if not totally, divorced from reality. But from the early nineteenth century, when ethnology began to emerge as a science in its own right, myth has become one of the most potentially creative concepts for an understanding of culture and civilisation, old and new.

Initially, myth comes alive in story, whereby the narrator portrays a state of affairs which brings an element of meaning and cohesion into the ambivalence and ambiguity of daily life. The myth-maker works on the creative imagination, not just the individual one, but what we may call the 'cosmic imagination' (which would closely resemble Jung's *collective unconscious* – *see* chapter 3) that conglomeration of hopes, fears and aspirations which, over the centuries, has become part of the primordial meaning-system of humankind. Describing the myth of primitive man, B.Malinowski (pp. 108, 110) provides us with what may serve as a working definition:

> Studied alive, myth. . . is not an explanation in satisfaction of a scientific interest, but an narrative resurrection of a primeval reality, told in satisfaction of deep, religious wants, moral cravings, social submissions, assertions, even practical requirements. Myth fulfils in primitive culture an indispensible function: it expresses, enhances and codifies belief; it safeguards and enforces morality; it vouches for the efficiency of ritual and contains practical rules for the guidance of man. Myth is thus a vital ingredient of human civilisation, it is not an idle tale but a hard-worked active force; it is not an intellectual explanation or an artistic imagery, but a pragmatic charter of primitive faith and moral wisdom. These stories. . . are to the natives a statement of a primeval, greater and more relevant reality, by which the present life, fates and activities of mankind are determined, the knowledge of which supplies man with the motive for ritual and moral actions, as well as with indications as to how to perform them.

In large measure myth has to do with *beginnings*. The world, myself, reality – how, when, why and where did it all begin? We notice that every developed civilisation has inherited a recorded set of primeval experiences, predating earliest historical records, defying logical and scientific explanation, subject, it would appear, to no known means of verification and yet captivating the minds and hearts of generations past and present:

> As a type of story, myths deal with cosmic and exemplary time, rather than historical time. The subject matter of myth is primeval origins,

ancestral models and paradigmatic lives, or expectations about the future and the end of time. Cosmic time stands outside history, beyond the reach of eye-witnesses and is thus inaccessible except through the imaginative and revelatory dimensions of sacred expression. Primeval origin stories, such as the Polynesian tale that the universe, including the gods, originated from an egg, and those from the book of Genesis that speak of Yahweh's creation of the world in six days, the expulsion of Adam and Eve from the garden of Eden and the confusion of tongues at the tower of Bable, are examples of myth.

. . . Myths are thus not only cosmological but ontological – that is, concerned with the condition and being of human existence. The ontological character of myth is evident in such themes as our original state, experiences of alienation or separation, and the origin of death and suffering (Roger Schmidt, pp 127, 128).

These mythic tales have a certain similarity, transcending time and culture, and depict a state of affairs reminiscent of the final harmony and bliss to which people aspire, rather than an original state of chaos out of which our world progressively evolved. Therefore, the narrator, and subsequently the recorders of these tales, seeks to transcend the present and project his listeners into a higher level of consciousness – a universal consciousness and, yet, one that resonates quite strongly with ordinary human awareness, even as experienced by our primitive ancestors. Whether the tales were real, imaginary, fictitious or legendary, seems to have mattered little; it is distinctly possible that such categories based on a segregation of the human and mental faculties, did not exist in primitive times. Instead people perceived, understood and grasped reality in holistic terms as is obvious in their close affinity with nature and their original perception of God as a God of wind and thunder, a God who lived with their dead and also in some sense in their own midst.

Mythology, therefore, is the root and essence of primitive belief, and while primitive religious systems are probably our strongest repositories of ancient mythology, they are by no means the only ones. Mythology permeates all aspects of culture and civilisation – in every age of man. There is no age without its myths; indeed, there is no age that does not live in its myths.

Starting, therefore, with the beginnings of life, early myth-makers continued to formulate tales explaining the mysteries of their lives and the world they inhabited. Sometimes, myths are associated with sages, enlightened individual men or women who interpreted experience for the benefit of all mankind. In its origins, however, myth is much more likely to have arisen from a collective, reflective experience, based initially on primitive story-telling and later on ritualistic and religious ceremonies.

Myth and Transcendence

Where did the mythical 'knowledge' come from? One attempts to answer this question by posing another: where does any artistic discovery come from, whether poetry, art or music? Perhaps, from the collective unconscious (Jung), those universally, shared (unarticulated) beliefs, feelings and emotions common to all members of our species. And this response begs another question: What is unique to the human person whereby it can respond to this experience in a mythical way? To this question we can give a variety of answers: Mind, imagination, spirit, soul, mentation. Rather than name any one specific faculty perhaps, we can focus on the human ability to *transcend*, to reach out, to grow beyond, to aspire towards a fuller and richer sense of wholeness. *Myth arises from transcendence*. It arises from within humanity, individually and collectively. It arises from a depth of human feeling and conviction untapped, as yet, by human knowledge. In the depth of the human heart lies a life-principle, restless in its urge to expand, precipitated towards a realisation knowing no limits, sometimes achieved in mystical experiencs, inner peace, sexual orgasm, but never totally experienced or appropriated. And it is as old as humanity itself; indeed, it may well be the core of human nature.

To deal with transcendence, human beings first invented mythology and then, religion. One uses the word *invent* with some caution because while early man invested his being, knowledge and feeling in the creation of myth, there is also a sense in which myth arose from within. Transcendence of its very nature seeks expression in human, earthly form. It cannot hold itself in a state of primordial abeyance; like all lifeforms its nature is to expand and evolve. Spirit is not alien to matter. Only matter informed by spirit can give life, and spirit without matter is merely an illusion.

Spirit, bursting forth, transcending its human and earthly habitat, creates the myth that brings meaning and purpose into human and earthly life. Transcendence, therefore, is not escapism; it is growth from within, transforming everything without and redirecting life on the path of interiority. Consequently the human person is the benign benefactor of an inevitable transcendence, to which he can give a positive or negative response. For the greater part of his evolution man has responded positively and creatively to the invitation to transcendence. There have been dark ages when humankind responded negatively to this invitation and, sadly, we in the northern hemisphere seem to be living in one such dark period of history (cf. Fritjof Capra, *The Turning Point*, pp. 248-281)

In terms of traditional religious concepts, the invitation to transcendence has the following implications:

1. The human being originates from both a physical and spiritual source, aptly and powerfully symbolised in the procreative, sexual encounter of man and woman, wherein both 'life-givers' are engulfed in the rapture of orgasmic union, an event, when appropriately experienced is profoundly spiritual as well as physical. In the human sexual encounter human beings share something of the primeval life-giving spirit, transforming 'nothingness' into being. Every human procreative act is willy nilly a cosmic event and enhances (or jeopardises) the course of evolution. The creative God and the creative person are one in the bestowal of life.

From the moment of conception man is inhabited by a *God-within*; we do not have to wait for the purifying waters of Christian baptism to allow the spirit inhabit the 'soul' of man. In the very act of creation God is present. Every created thing is a reflection of its creator, including man, the apex of creation. Therefore, all people, irrespective of race, creed or colour are children of God. We inhabit and are inhabited by the-God-within, ever inviting us to respond to the gift of life in whose evolutionary growth we are called to participate. The *transcendence-seeking-expression* is nothing less than the spirit of God (by whatever name one chooses to use) continually seeking to become flesh (to become incarnate) in our lives and, through us, in our world.

2. Human beings are, therefore, *naturally* spiritual. The propensity to transcend and make contact with life beyond our own personalities and environment is a natural endowment, which, in its very outward reach also strives for inner depth at the level of the individual person. Along with the physical, social and psychic dimensions of the human personality we postulate the *spiritual*. We venture further and suggest that the spiritual is the ultimate and most pervasive force for harmony, maturity and integration in

human beings; this observation is made solely on anthropological evidence, exemplified in man's long history striving to 'communicate' with God, as expressed in the vast array of mythology, ritual and worship, produced throughout the ages of human life on this earth.

3. Next, we draw an important distinction between the *spiritual* and the *religious* aspect of human life. Every human being is spiritual, but not necessarily religious. The desire and tendency to transcend belongs to humankind for some 100,000 years and its growth and expression, while determined by many human factors, has not been inhibited by them. In other words, the spiritual aspiration of Neanderthal man was expressed in symbolic imagery and narration, appropriate to humanity at that stage of development and, therefore, in a different, but not inferior, way to that of man at the *Homo Sapiens* stage. And in the sophisticated 'advanced' world of today, we too express our spiritual identity in myths and rituals of our own making, very different from those of our primitive ancestors, but not superior to them – because it is the same basic needs we are striving to serve and articulate.

One is not suggesting that man's spirituality remains somehow stable and unchanged. The need for spiritual growth is unique for every member of the species at every moment in history, nor does one wish to suggest a certain uniformity because it is elicited by the one God we are all seeking to serve. No, we simply wish to establish the spiritual dimension of human nature, which like the physical, social and psychic has existed through all the ages of man, changing in so far as it is continually growing and developing and, therefore, always seeking and making possible for itself new forms of expression (i.e. new myths).

Spiritual man existed for some 70,000 years before religious man (strictly so called) came to the fore. Hinduism is the first major world religion to emerge, dated at about 2000 BC. Between that time and 1500 AD, a time span of 3,500 years (which is a mere second in the time-scale of human evolution), some ten major religious systems, all surviving today, came into existence. The reasons for this major religious upsurge at that point in time are outlined on p. 18 above. At this juncture, one wishes merely to establish that religious man is a relatively recent visitor to our planet and while the establishment of religious systems may be considered to be spiritually progressive (many argue to the contrary), it is not appropriate to suggest that religious man is a better spiritual person than his non-religious predecessors. The quality of faith and practice among our primitive ancestors was unique to and appropriate for their time and culture and, within their own context, they must be considered as genuinely and sincerely spiritual as any adherent of a formal religion today.

4. Are our religious systems, therefore, superfluous? One cannot answer that question with a simple *Yes* or *No*. With the progressive development of human civilisation it is conceivable that human beings at some stage would have formalised and socialised their spiritual beliefs and customs. We do not understand why this was done in the time and manner of its implementation. As already intimated it seems to coincide with the evolution of self-awareness in the human species which in turn enhanced the spiritual maturity of humankind.

Yet, this development has not been without its hazards and, even, its tragedies. In many parts of the world, official religion has become so formalised, so legalised in its norms and expectations, that man's underlying spiritual nature (which can survive without any formal religion) is completely overshadowed. Religion often serves and thrives on unarticulated, ideological convictions rather than on genuine spiritual aspirations. Peoples' genuine faith and their formal religious practice are often poles apart. Sadder still are the numerous people in our world who religiously follow one or other formal system but spiritually worship gods of this world, whether power, glory, achievement, etc. Their sense of transcendence is often more clearly felt in the latter than the former. The reader need not be reminded of the several occasions in recent human history where religion became the justifying cause for torture, warfare and gross human manipulation (more on this in chapter 6). So whither religion – a blessing or a bane?

5. Let us look at our response to the invitation to transcendence in today's world. As humans beings, we all need a 'God' to believe in, an ulterior motive or cause which urges us on to the heights of our inner greatness as spiritual beings. In today's world there are many gods, most of them false and not a few belonging to formal religious systems. For many people, money, power, prestige, have become the focal points for meaning and purpose in their lives; take away these

props, that is, kill the gods, and their world falls apart. For others the exploitation of the human body, especially the female body, is an issue of passionate importance for those whose 'god' is pleasure, drugs, drink, sex, the erotic, etc., and strange as it may seem, the believers of this creed include many women! Others, disillusioned with the gods of this world, but also with the gods of formal religion, turn to various forms of meditation, relaxation techniques and a variety of psychological and pseudo-psychological approaches to achieve inner peace. These trends are often pejoratively described as 'the cult of self' (cf. Paul C. Vitz). It is an unfortunate castigation because the many followers today searching for this inward God whether through T.M., Silva Mind Control, psychedelic drugs, in-depth meditation or even Charismatic Renewal may be much more in tune with the contemporary evolution of the human species than many of the so-called 'normal' people in our society.

Then we have the gods of formal religion, the true God for many people, but in practice a God who is often used in moments of difficulty or trouble but rarely thanked or praised, a God who becomes all important in the official place of worship but is comfortably ignored in the market place, so that we can cheat and pilfer, perpetuate injustice and wholesale exploitation, a God we use to give us status and responsibility, a God who is convenient, easy to cope with, easy to keep at a safe distance. Formal religion has also produced that God in whose name, and for whose teaching, we have brutally murdered, maimed and exploited others, a God we have imposed on people of other races and cultures, a God we consider to be so superior that we have often savagely condemned and exterminated others to perpetuate his reign. Christians and Muslims and, in a more subtle way, Communists, are, or have been, the greatest proponents of such oppression. The God of formal religion, whom so many take to be the real God, is frequently only a caricature, an idol of our own making, a poor reflection of the living God.

Finally, we have those who claim they don't know God and cannot worship him, but never seem to be able to escape from his shadow. They often enjoy a good argument about God. They may quietly strive to discover God through philosophy, or disprove his existence through science. These are people who adopt the title *atheist* or *agnostic*, often as a defence-mechanism against the God who:

> 'Nigh and nigh draws the chase
> With unperturbed pace
> Deliberate speed, majestic instancy'
> — FRANCIS THOMPSON

Perhaps the greatest tribute we can pay these people is to acknowledge them as genuine searchers. To them, as to Pascal, God may well be saying: 'You wouldn't be searching for me unless you had already found me.' Yet, for many of these same people, the search may be lifelong. Paradoxically, they form a prophetic nucleus in our world, challenging on the one hand, those of us who blindly succumb to a false secular God (power, pleasure, prestige) and, on the other, those of us who worship the convenient, self-righteous God of formal religion, to come face to face with the true God who can never be an idol of our making but rather invites us to a continual growth and transformation of ourselves and our world. The atheists and the agnostics may well be the saviours of our civilisation (more on this in Chapter 9):

> Is it not the situation of many of us today that we feel we *must* be atheists. God, as we have been led to posit him, is intellectually superfluous, is emotionally dispensable and is morally intolerable – and yet, in grace and demand, he *will not* let us go. The hound of heaven still dogs us, the 'beyond in our midst' still encounters us, when all the images, all the projections, even all the words for God have been broken. . . God is a reality of life whom we cannot ultimately evade. . . The one who is superfluous as a hypothesis becomes all too present as a subject in encounter (John A. T. Robinson, pp. 115-119).

Our excursus into man's spiritual development and the emergence of formal religious systems, along with the distinction between the spiritual and the religious dimensions, enable us to analyse in greater depth the mythology of religion. Let us again recall that man's initial spiritual awareness emerged in story, a form of narration that strives to give meaning to life and its daily events. These stories, retained and retold, come to be known as *myths*.

The survival of myth thrives on a law common to all life forms: the cycle of life and death. A vibrant myth is time conditioned; its life-span is determined by many cultural and historical factors. It survives while it is serving genuine human needs; new needs generate new myths. Old myths may survive in an art form now called *folklore*. They may survive in another form – not always readily recognised, although potentially lethal to human progress – namely, *ideology*; to that topic we will later turn our attention.

Myth Expressed through Ritual

Myth, in its original form has an aura of novelty, discovery, meaning, purpose and value. The original story is more an articulation of the myth than an explanation of it and the story quickly develops from being a meaningful narration, worthy of attention and response, to a meaning-giving action demanding involvement and eventually commitment. What we call 'meaning-giving action' is known today as *ritual*. Historically, ritual was the second step in man's religious awareness, whereby he sought to express in *symbolic* action his need for God and, more important still, his felt need to be incorporated into God's activity in this life. In its most elementary form, ritual is a form of behaviour which connects us with the invisible world of the spirit and the unseen presence of God.

Ritual also has a powerful socialising capacity, enhancing the bonds already in existence, arising from the fellowship of story-telling and giving it new depth and cohesion:

> Ritual is one of the principal vehicles that binds people together in a community of shared interests and tradition. Ritual and ritual elements provide group-associational patterns through which people learn what is expected of them and to whom or what they belong. Communities are formed around and sustained by shared rites and symbols. Where common symbols are weak or non-existent an experience of community is unlikely. (Roger Schmidt, pp 162-163)

Today, we associate ritual almost exclusively with religious ceremony. Because our ceremonies and liturgies tend to be stylised and formalised, they fail to convey the emotion, feeling and conviction embodied in primitive ritual or indeed, in any ritualistic process – ancient or modern – in its initial stages. Many aspects of human behaviour have been and continue to be ritualised, especially those associated with significant, meaning-bearing events, such as marriages, funerals, state protocol. Traditional ritualistic behaviour and its role in society is much more apparent among African and Asian peoples and is resourcefully portrayed in symbolically endowed ritual.

Ritualised behaviour pertains to many aspects of human life, but tends to be more associated with religious behaviour. This observation merits attention because religious behaviour is no more dependent on ritual than any other aspect of human life. Ritual happens to have a closer affinity with religion precisely because religion touches (or, at least, is intended to touch) deeper layers of meaning in the human personality. Ritual is man's effort to put a structure and name on a quality of life that he wishes to own, retain and maintain, which he feels can only be done by systematising and structuring it; while this process is necessary, it poses a real threat to the survival of ritual, as we shall see presently.

Ritual and its significance in people's lives has·been extensively studied by anthropologists. Of particular interest for the present study is the work of Victor Turner who describes the ritual process as (a) beginning with a rite of separation, (b) entering a transition or liminal period and (c) concluding with an act of incorporation. Along with the anthropologists, depth-psychologists (especially of the Jungian line) point out that these three phases of the ritual process resemble three dimensions of an universal cosmic force present in all people, namely, *separation, initiation* and *return.* Illustrating this triadic structure, Schmidt (p. 178) uses the example of traditional Jewish marriage which had three distinctive stages: the *engagement* which set the prospective bride and groom apart from their traditional family circle; the *betrothal*, lasting about one year, a time of struggle, assessment and anticipation in which the consequences of marriage were faced and, finally the *marriage*, forming a new family nucleus and thus marking a return to one's original familial setting.

The triadic structure which, according to Turner, is marked by a dialectical movement from structure to anti-structure to a reincorporation of structure, features in many aspects of human life, especially in the departure from home and family circle, initiated by many people in late adolescence, solidified in establishing new relationships and employment for one's own survival and, finally, actualised in setting up one's own home, partnership and family. The process features strongly in every world religion, as exemplified in the Christian idea of the seed falling into the ground and dying in order to produce new life (cf. John 12:24), which, of course, serves only to highlight the biblical triad of Birth–Death–Rebirth (Resurrection).

Initially, therefore, ritual is neither a deliberately structured set of rites nor a haphazard sequence of symbolic behaviours. Rather, it seems to emerge as an experimental and spontaneous sequence of gestures, verbal and non-verbal, expressive of primeval, dialectical yearnings in the human person. Once a pattern of ritual has been established it quickly tends to become solidified in the hope of retaining the feelings of well-being and affirmation, experienced in the initial rites. Therefore, ritual reinforces social bonds and tends to become a powerfully unifying force for human groups, more noticeably, perhaps, in primitive times than in our own day.

What do rituals consist of? Basically, they comprise a repertoire of symbolic words and gestures which lift the participant out of the greyness and ordinarinesss of daily existence into a more integrated level of feeling and awareness, whereby daily experience is transcended and simultaneously transformed (i.e. given new meaning). Ritual in its pure form is not escapist; in transcending one's daily lot the participant returns to the earthly task revitalised, re-animated and recommitted. The ordinary tasks are seen in a new light, given new meaning, absorbed into a new feeling of direction and purpose. This transformatory experience was probably much more real for our primitive ancestors than for many people today committed to official religion.

The symbolic content of primitive ritual merits some attention. Eric Werner believes that worship may have originated in the sacred cries which primitive cults emitted for the purpose of inviting friendly forces and warding off demonic ones. A symbolic act which consists of action (gesture, sound or body position) and ordinary objects (such as bread, wine, water) sets out to re-interpret reality from the perspective of man's inner world of imagination, intuition, ecstasy, emotion and inner wholeness. Therefore, a national flag, although merely a piece of cloth, and standing to attention as just another body-position, when taken out of their symbolic context, where they confer meaning and transform consciousness, create cohesion and elicit what at times can be a highly charged emotional response. Human beings are 'meaning-conferring' creatures, without which capacity they would be unable to survive as human beings.

It is precisely when human beings fail to dream and express their aspirations in a creative and symbolic way that irrational tendencies come to the fore. In symbolic behaviour we create outlets for deep-seated emotions, positive and negative. It is worthy of note that animals rarely kill their own species because conflict tends to ensue in highly ritualistic behaviour in which the negative energy dissipates. Anthropological evidence also suggests that primitive man, for whom ritual was very important, was not nearly as cruel to his own or other life-forms as popular opinion maintains. 'The truth is,' claims John Gribben (p. 295), 'our hunting ancestors led much more peaceful lives than the first farmers – the blame for warfare can be laid at the door of agriculture, not on the shoulders of ancestral hunters.'

The twentieth century marks new levels in man's inhumanity to man. Could it be that this has resulted from excessive rationalism, whereby all that pertains to man's symbolic and spiritual existence has been suppressed by the emerging scientific consciousness, believing only in what can be objectively proved and verified!

Within human beings is an universal propensity for the symbolic as a vehicle of purpose and meaning. However, symbolic behaviour is also culturally determined and usually expressed in the language and gesture of each ethnic or cultural group. The history of symbolic expression is very complex and must, on the one hand, recognise the possibility of universal symbols, matching the Jungian archetypes (see pp. 55-56) and therefore common to all humanity and, on the other, localised symbols, pertaining to specific cultural groupings. In this distinction may we not have the basis for the major world religions, all obviously devoted to the exploration of man's search for meaning but each approaching its task with a distinctive uniqueness. We will return to this topic in chapter 7.

In resumé let us recall once again the central role of story-telling for our primitive ancestors. From these stories emerged myths, tales which explained and gave meaning to life, a process which spontaneously led to acting-out the story and hence the creation of ritual, highlighting the power and potential of the symbolic for the human species. At this stage we encounter the negative side of human nature which paradoxically points to one of our deepest needs and aspirations, namely, the human urge to control and institutionalise one's achievements. Therefore, ritualistic ceremonies which enriched and enhanced human life tended to become structured and stabilised on the presumption that this would facilitate their repetition and prolong their ability to confer meaning and purpose. Thus rituals became official ceremonies, stylised and formalised and these mark the beginnings of primitive belief systems.

Any attempt to date the above process is both pointless and inappropriate: pointless because we lack the necessary historical and anthropological data; inappropriate because we can presume that the process repeated itself many times, in different parts of the world, in keeping with human evolutionary emergence. Man's interest in religion, as gleaned from the cave drawings of Upper Paleolithic times (35,000-10,000 BC), especially those discovered in the caves of Lascaux, Altamira and Pech-Merle, all dated around 15,000 BC, mark a highly developed stage of primitive religious awareness. The religious consciousness exemplified in Ice Age art marks the high point of an evolutionary process unfolding over some 40,000 years of man's existence on earth.

Although we encounter a high-point of religious consciousness between 15,000 and 10,000 BC, it is difficult to conceive of any formal religious system before 3,500 BC, when the first written religious texts (the Summerian texts) were compiled. Our first record of temple building is from the same time, c. 3,600 BC. And the first formal religious system, Hinduism, emerges about 2,000 BC.

The Threat of Ideology

Religion, therefore, even in its formal sense, is essentially *mythological*; in other words, its primary purpose is to connect people with the basic human search for *meaning*, as articulated by human beings down through the ages in story, ritual and worship. This 'basic human search' is the spiritual thirst of humanity for an integrated and coherent comprehension of life; it expresses a profound human need to hold together in some type of creative synthesis, the polarities and contradictions of human experience.

No one religious system can contain and express this synthesis to the satisfaction of all people. Consequently, a variety of religious systems have come into being and such a variety is likely to prevail. Furthermore, within each system is a diversity of religious awareness, experience and motivation, which a system can only hold together in a loose and flexible structure. But systems have an inherent tendency towards fixity and institutionalisation (cf. chapter 6) which limit and even hinder their usefulness. When this tendency towards institutionalisation becomes so pronounced that one particular institutional expression becomes the only acceptable one, to which all adherents are expected to give allegiance, then we are dealing with *ideology*.

It is relatively easy to recognise ideological influences. The norms, rules and regulations of one particular expression of the religious search take on an absolute and unchangeable character. The temporary vehicle of meaning has become permanent and absolute. Non-conformists are considered to be dangerous and tend to be eased-out in devious and pernicious ways. Strong defence mechanisms ensure that new ideas and challenges are kept at a safe distance. The new institution becomes virtually impermeable. Religion has become an ideology, wherein man's conscious effort after meaning has become unconsciously identified with one particular expression of the religious quest.

In today's world, much of what we call religion is really ideology. Some classic examples of ideology in its extreme form include the brand of Christianity espoused by Rev. Ian Paisley and his followers in Northern Ireland; the Islamic belief of the Ayotollah Kohmeini in Iran or the Guyana massacre of 1978. In all these situations people feel so emotionally bonded to one particular religious institution that they are no longer free within themselves to evaluate it objectively or even determine what purpose it serves for them. On the surface, religious expression may seem deep and authentic, but real spiritual growth has ceased; people have become fixated and arrested at one particular point of their emotional and spiritual development. In this state, they can easily succumb to pernicious, subversive and irrational influences as can easily be detected in the examples quoted above.

Every religious system seeks to express an underlying myth, a story which seeks to articulate and convey meaning. What is really important is not the religion but the myth. Because human beings change (growth-in-maturity cannot happen without change), myth has to change if it is to facilitate growth in an ongoing, coherent and integrating way. If this change is inhibited or prevented then the myth becomes warped and distorted, usually in one of two ways:

(a) When myth is considered to be primitive and inferior and, therefore, not appropriate for the scientific and rational mind of the twentieth century. In this case, people are inadvertently creating a new myth which is often called the *scientific attitude*. Because this new myth seeks to exclude a spiritual dimension, thus ignoring an integral aspect of human life, it is destined to become more baffling and oppressive than the one people are seeking to dispense with. In fact, the myth we call 'scientific attitude' may already be in decline (see chapter 8).

(b) When the myth has outlived its usefulness; this tends to happen when myth is confused with historical fact, as in the Genesis story of Creation in six days. The Genesis account is fundamentally a story, seeking to confer meaning. Whether the facts are true or not was immaterial to the people who initially heard and shared the story. In the light of evolutionary knowledge the story may not be appropriate today to confer the meaning initially intended. The need for this meaning still prevails and will continue while human beings inhabit our world. To satisfy the contemporary search for meaning, the story must be retold in language and concepts appropriate to the people of our time. If the story cannot be retold because of a perceived betrayal or denial of orthodox ecclesiastical teaching, then the Church is operating out of an ideology rather than out of genuine religion.

Because of unconscious elements, ideologies tend to be very powerful. They can survive for centuries, halting real spiritual growth and fostering attitudes of bigotry and fanaticism, sometimes in extreme forms. Every formal religion runs the risk of becoming an ideology. Religious systems such as Roman Catholicism and Islam, which demand strong allegiance to those in authority and tend to hold a tight reign on new ideas and experiments, are particularly conducive to ideological influence. In such cases, the religious system tends to become a power-structure and, perhaps, a status symbol, commanding allegiance through coercion rather than through inspiration.

Latin-American theologian, Gustavo Gutierrez (pp. 234-235) conscious of the ideological religious trends in his own continent, says:

> Ideology has a long and varied history and has been understood in different ways. But we can basically agree that ideology does not offer adequate and scientific knowledge of reality; rather, *it masks it* (emphasis mine). Ideology does not rise above the empirical, irrational level. Therefore, it spontaneously fulfils a function of preservation of the established order (and) . . . tends to dogmatise all that has not succeeded in separating itself from it or has fallen under its influence, . . . and faith does not escape this danger.

On the other hand, sociologist, Daniel Bell, argues for the 'end of ideology', claiming that today old ideologies are exhausted and nothing has emerged to take their place. There may be truth in this observation precisely because we are living at a time of major cultural transition where traditional values, including ideologies, no longer command a strong allegiance. But as Karl Mannheim has convincingly demonstrated, ideology is not a set of behaviour-patterns dominating a specific group or culture, but rather a dimension of *knowledge* often embodied in the unarticulated assumptions which govern both our values and behaviour.

Just as there is no age or culture without its myths there is none either without its ideologies. The former express man's sense of originality and his capacity to dream, invent and create and the latter reminds us of the human need for security, stability, and control of the environment. While a healthy culture demands a balance between the two, it is an unfortunate fact of history that the emphasis has been largely on the latter, an observation which in itself should motivate us toward a a more conscious cultivation of the former.

Ideologies, as already stated, are self-perpetuating, governed largely by the collective unconscious which reinforces the power of the underlying belief to create greater group cohesion and greater allegiance to group values. Thus, ideology and institutionalisation become synonymous, forming an almost impenetrable structure that can provide tremendous security, but also extreme reaction in the face of challenge or investigation. The Guyana massacre of 1978 serves as a good example of how extremely dangerous religion can become and how potentially counterproductive the institutionalisation of religion can be.

In chapter 6, we outline the social potency of religion in both its positive and negative aspects. An institutional structure is an indispensible requisite for the practice of religion. Religion is inherently social as well as personal; one's faith can only be authentically personal when it is shared with one's fellow human beings. Religion, therefore, needs a social structure, an institutional form. Unfortunately, the human tendency is to cling to established structures -- initially, because they embody the shared vision of the participants, but as time advances, mainly because of the security and stability they offer. If an institution is to faithfully reflect its initial purpose it must remain continually open to the *change* necessitated by new understandings of the original myth, new ideas arising from this growth, new procedures to express these ideas in action, and new ways for the group to celebrate together their new identity. Mature religion can only thrive in such a growing, changing environment.

The fact that religion today is irrelevant for some and confusing for others, and thus failing to touch in depth the majority of people, is convincing proof that the institutions in which our religious ideals are embodied have become lifeless and archaic. It is the perpetual threat of all institutions, and although it has happened several times in the course of history, we are still loath to accept (or even acknowledge) the consequences.

Religion today is out of touch with its myth, with the goal of its transcendence. The dominant religion is either the institutionalised form that is crumbling – not just in the west, but in other cultures too – or the secular religion of modern science (based on values of power, control, prestige and instant pleasure) which, in the past ten years, has lost the good favour even of some of its own disciples. Fritjof Capra claims that the scientific revolution, based on what he calls the *Cartesian-Newtonian mechanistic* view of life is also approaching its end as a new scientific myth based on a *holistic* paradigm is gradualy emerging:

> In contrast to the mechanistic, Cartesian view of the world, the world view emerging from modern physics can be characterised by words like organic, holistic and ecological. . . The universe is no longer seen as a machine, made up of a multitude of objects, but has to be pictured as one, indivisible, dynamic whole whose parts are essentially interrelated, and can be understood only as patterns of a cosmic process. (*The Turning Point*, p. 66)

Myths do not die easily; as new perceptions of reality arise within a culture, the old fades into the background, becoming increasingly irrelevant and antiquated. Although no longer useful, entrenched myths (i.e. ideologies) can exert a very powerful influence, creating divisiveness and polarisation. Such resistence becomes particularly stubborn when the new myth is seen to arise more from outside the official churches than from within. Such is the case today: the *holistic systems* paradigm, of which more will be said throughout this book, is articulated most powerfully in physics, biology, ecology, psychology, medicine and economics. So far, theology, apart from the pioneering work of Teilhard de Chardin and a few other isolated efforts, has not caught up with this new movement.

The credibility of the new myth rests with its evolutionary sense, not with its scientific verifiability. Its global vision, its powerful unifying dynamic, its integration of all life-dimensions including the spiritual (mystical), its transcending momentum beyond the physical to the psychic – the main focal point of contemporary, evolutionary growth – all give the new orientation a strength and durability which is sure to endure. As the new myth unfolds, abandoning the outdated and irrelevant trimmings of the past, a new religious consciousness will also transpire. Externally, it may or may not, have much in common with earlier forms. It is not the external expression, however, but the inner motivation, which will awaken a new sense of exploration, reconnecting us with two important points of origin: our *primordial, human heritage,* explored in chapter 1 and the present chapter and our *individual inner core of meaning,* to which we will now turn our attention.

Bibliography

Campbell, Joseph, *The Masks of God: Primitive Mythology,* The Viking Press, 1959.

Capra, Fritjof, *The Turning Point,* Flamingo/Fontana, 1982.

Eliade, Mircea, *The Quest: History and Meaning in Religion,* University of Chicago Press, 1969.

——, *Man and the Sacred,* Harper & Row, 1974.

Gutierrez, Gustavo, *A Theology of Liberation,* SCM Press, 1974.

Malinowski, B., *Magic, Science and Religion,* New York, 1955.

Mannheim, Karl, *Ideology and Utopia,* Routledge & Kegan Paul, 1960.

Robinson, J. A. T., *The New Reformation,* SCM Press, 1965.

Schmidt, Roger, *Exploring Religion,* California, Wadsworth, 1980.

Shea, John, *Stories of Faith,* Chicago: The Thomas More Press, 1980.

Smart, Ninian, *The Concept of Worship,* Macmillan Press, 1972.

Turner, Victor, *The Ritual Process,* Chicago: Aldine, 1968.

Vitz, Paul, C., *Psychology as Religion: The Cult of Self-Worship,* Lion paperback, 1977.

Wach, Joachim, *The Comparative Study of Religions,* Columbia University Press, 1958.

3

The Human Capacity for Belief
(Psychology)

The man who regards his life as meaningless is not merely unhappy, but hardly fit for life. — ALBERT EINSTEIN

Man projects ultimate meanings into reality because reality is, indeed, ultimately meaningful. — PETER BERGER

If the doors of perception were cleansed, everything would appear to man as it is, infinite. — WILLIAM BLAKE

WILLIAM JAMES, one of the father-figures of modern psychology devoted an entire volume, *Varieties of Religious Experience* to the study of the human religious aspiration, wherein he wrote the following words:

The perfect stillness of the night was thrilled by a more solemn silence. The darkness held a presence that was all the more felt because it was not seen. I could not anymore have doubted that *He* was there than that I was. Indeed, I felt myself to be, if possible, the less real of the two (pp. 66-67).

Quoting Tolstoy approvingly, James wrote in the same book:

Since mankind has existed, wherever life has been, there also has been the faith that gave the possibility of living. Faith is the sense of life, that sense by virtue of which man does not destroy himself, but continues to live on. It is the force whereby we live. If man did not believe that he must live for something, he would not live at all. The idea of an infinite God, of the divinity of the soul, of the union of men's actions with God — these are ideas elaborated in the infinite secret depths of human thought. They are ideas without which there would be no life, without which I myself. . . would not exist. I began to see that I had no right to rely on my individual reasoning and neglect these answers given by faith, for they are the only answers to the question.

While sociology examines observable, social behaviour and the interaction of that behaviour within various social systems and with society at large, psychology seeks to explore the *motivation* generating such behaviour in the first place. Human beings tend to behave in accordance with the accepted expectations of society. Behind this apparent conformity, however, is a plethora of motivating factors which in traditional, Freudian terms may be *conscious* (those of which we are aware), *preconscious* (those we can choose to bring into our awareness) or *subconscious* (unknown, but often profoundly affecting our behaviour). It is the task of the psychologist of religion to uncover man's reason for positing and maintaining belief in a transcendent reality called, 'God' and to establish (if possible) whether the origin of this desire has a basis in reality or is merely a creation of the human imagination.

William James asserted that the religious aspiration is inherent to human nature (even to man's physical survival) and the God we postulate is for James a real God with whom human beings can relate in a real, though super-empirical way. Freud, who probed the recesses of the psyche at a depth far exceeding that of James, took quite a different view. For Freud, religion was an illusion, in which a father-figure is created imaginatively in order to fulfil a psychoanalytic wish to make tolerable the helplessness of man:

> For there is nothing new in this situation. It has an infantile prototype, and is really only the continuation of this. For once before one has been in such a state of helplessness: as a little child in relationship to one's parents. For one had reason to fear them, especially the father, though at the same time one was sure of his protection against the dangers then known to one. And so it was natural to assimilate and combine the two situations. Here, too, as in dream life, the wish came into its own (*The Future of an Illusion*, p. 29).

Religion, therefore, is a coping mechanism, but in Freud's view, an infantile one which man should discard and, instead, face the hopelessness and helplessness of life as an adult, reconciling himself to the inevitable meaninglessness of it all.

Karl Marx held a somewhat similar view:

> In fact, religion is simply the awareness that man has of himself. However, man is not an abstract being wandering outside this world. Man

is the human world, the state, society. It is the state and society that produces religion. Religion is the inversion of the conceptual world precisely because this world is in fact inverted (*Early Writings,* p. 43).

Marx goes on to argue that people use religion as an opiate against the pain and suffering of society. We can only get rid of such misery by first abandoning the 'crutch' which, in the first place, compels us to tolerate suffering. Consequently,

> . . . the abolition of religion in so far as it is the illusory happiness of human beings, is required for their happiness. The call to abandon the illusions of their conditions is a call to abandon a condition which requires illusion. Hence, the criticism of religion is, in germ, the criticism of this vale of tears of which religion is the crown (*Early Writings,* p. 44).

For Marx, the answer to human alienation rests in the ability of society to take possession of all the means of production and use them intelligently for the benefit of all. In this way, man can be redeemed from the bondage created by his illusory allegiance to spiritual forces, who only help to maintain the helplessness of the human condition.

Both Freud and Marx reflected a mode of thought arising from the logical positivism and existentialist philosophy of the late nineteenth century, which maintained that meaninglessness and alienation were part of the human condition for which man had no remedy. Religion, therefore, was essentially a projection of human nature into the beyond in order to escape the inevitable confrontation with the confusion and uncertainty of life. Ludwig Feuerbach, one of the outstanding proponents of this view, wrote: 'Man – this is the mystery of religion – projects his being into objectivity, and then again makes himself an object to this projected image of himself thus converted into a subject. . . God is the highest subjectivity of man abstracted from himself (*The Essence of Christianity,* pp. 13-14).

In more recent times J. A. T. Robinson has used the idea of projection in connection with the concept of the 'God of the gaps', the God we human beings employ to resolve challenges we either fear or wish to escape. Behaviourist psychology (i.e. the Watson and Skinner tradition) has consistently refused to accommodate religious belief in its analysis of human behaviour, deeming it to be a fictitious creation of man's imagination, potentially more destructive than constructive in getting people to take responsibility for the quality of human life.

With good reason, psychology down to our own day, treats religion with basic suspicion and mistrust. Many psychological disorders are known to arise from excessive guilt or piety on either one's own part or through the influence of family and/or close associates. Fanatical and immature religious beliefs have often hindered mature growth and development. Official churches, especially in the Christian tradition, have viewed psychology sceptically and sometimes with downright scorn and condemnation.

This, of course, is only one side of the story. Psychology's positive contribution to the understanding of religion is enormous and will be examined presently. However, we do not wish to lose sight of the combined insights of Feuerbach, Freud and Marx because they highlight a truth none of us wish to face, namely, that religion can be, and often is, an escape from reality, a mode of recourse to a 'God-out-there' whom we use as the occasion fits, often to bolster our unwillingness (perhaps, our sloth) to take appropriate, human initiatives, to explain away ambiguities *we* should strive to resolve or, perhaps, worst of all, to align ourselves socially with certain classes or groups of people. Adherence to religious duties, rites and obligations often arises more from a fear of law or a fear of the consequences of non-conformity rather than from genuine, personal conviction. It is the task of the psychologist to unearth these ambivalent and negative motivations so that people can examine them in openness and truth.

Religion and Psychological Needs

In 1964, M. Argyle published a short essay outlining what he considered to be the main psychological roots for religious beliefs:

1. *Direct need-reduction:* Religion may be used as a substitute for deficiences in one's life, especially those associated with fear, guilt or anxiety, as experienced by people of every race and culture. These needs may be more strongly felt among 'uneducated and primitive people', but this does not validate Argyle's conclusion that religion as a need-fulfilment mechanism was more widely used by our primitive ancestors than by our contemporaries. What Argyle and psychologists generally have failed to perceive is the nature and origin of the need articulated in, and satisfied by, religious belief. Indeed, contemporary psychology may not have the tools to explore this dimension of the human psyche, at least, not while it takes its

terms of reference largely or exclusively from a mechanistic-scientific paradigm of human nature. Once we acknowledge a spiritual dimension as being inherent to the human personality, a conclusion which seems inescapable for the anthropologist and increasingly for the exponents of all branchs of science, then we can no longer opt for religion being merely the reduction of need (except, perhaps, on some overt level) but rather the expression and articulation of a primeval and eternal dimension of human life itself.

2. *Anxiety Reduction:* According to Argyle, situations that are a source of stress and anxiety can be rendered harmless by the adoption of certain beliefs about them. He substantiates this statement with the research of Malinowski, Spiro, Pfister and others – studies carried out among modern primitive tribes in which overt behaviour is presumed to be an accurate reflection of internal motivation. Primitive man's creation of religious ritual may have sought the reduction of anxiety as a subconscious rather than conscious choice, but the main purpose of such ritual was the creation of a coherent, meaningful existence. The ultimate goal of religion is positive and constructive. Man as a *creature of meaning* and a *bearer of meaning,* continually seeks to give meaning to, and extrapolate meaning from the ambiguities of life. Underlying all ritual and religious behaviour is a primordial will-to-meaning (Frankl), arising from a primeval conviction that life is ultimately meaningful.

3. *Internal Conflict:* Argyle rightly points to the tendency in both Catholicism and Protestantism (and to some extent in all religions) to create guilt feelings in the name of a theology largely focused on sin and salvation. What he fails to acknowledge is the underlying myth (again, common to all religions) whereby terms like 'sin' and 'salvation' have become the doctrinal (theological) tools by which we name a fundamental struggle in human nature, since the beginning of man's creation. It is wrong to suggest, therefore, that religion causes the guilt and conflict. It may intensify the feeling and sometimes prolong it even to neurotic or psychotic levels, but it does not create it. Take away religion completely and the human being will still grapple with an emptiness-within, an inescapable aloneness and feeling of alienation.

4. *God as Fantasy, Parent-Figure:* Here we touch on the Freudian projections in which the punitive father looms large. The catecheti-

cal tendency of identifying God as a fatherly type, may have some undesirable psychological consequences depending on the model of fatherhood employed. That God can become a fantasy, 'escape-mechanism' is undoubtedly true and many people have used and continue to use religion as an escape from life. All these observations, however, pertain to cultural conditioning rather than to the development of religious awareness and belief. Again, we are dealing with the overt, observable symptoms rather than with the real phenomenon.

5. *Ego Identity:* Here Argyle is touching a keystone in the development of religious awareness. However, because of his apparent unfamiliarity with anthropology on the one hand, and more recent work on the psychology of religion, on the other, his analysis is somewhat superficial. The identity found in one or other religious systems can be quite superficial although, on the surface, very impressive. People of evangelical upbringing can be quite articulate and forceful in quoting scripture and applying it to life, yet, can be extremely intolerant and even bigoted towards others, even of their own religious persuasion. Achieving mature ego-identity, religion being a significant component, tends to integrate religion into one's total life-project, maintaining an openness and flexibility of belief and custom, even to the extent of changing from one religion to another. One is not suggesting that this is necessarily a sign of, or a prerequisite for, religious maturity, but a sense of flexibility, openness, and lack of rigid dogmatism are certainly qualities of a mature faith. Therefore, the term 'ego-identity' when used in a religious context, is synonymous not merely with a depth of conviction but also with a breadth of vision.

6. *Cognitive Clarity: the Need for Understanding:* In varying degrees, religion enables people to understand life. Religion has a strong cognitive component and a continual flaw of religious protagonists is to uphold the cognitive to the detriment of the experiential. Here again, anthropology comes to our rescue: initially, religion arose from man's felt needs in the experience of daily life; it was not thought out or expressed in dogma or definitive structure. In fact, the cognitive elements only came to the fore with the establishment of formal religious systems and, today, dominate Roman Catholicism and other religions to varying degrees. Despite these negative assertions, Argyle is correct in drawing our attention to the cognitive

elements, because at this stage in evolution *mind* (what others call *mentation*) has become a focal point for evolutionary growth giving the human cognitive faculty a power for transcendence and integration probably not available to the human species in former times.

7. *Biochemical Factors:* Experiments with Mescaline and LSD, or meditation techniques, seeking altered states of consciousness, have led some researchers to suggest that there may be a biochemical component in religious experience. The expression of religious feelings in such states obviously depends on earlier religious influences, either personally or culturally. It is difficult to imagine that intervention in biochemical processes – solely at that level – could, in itself, generate religious awareness. However, the suggestion has some merit and cannot be quickly dismissed. If the different processes of the human personality (physical, social, psychic, spiritual etc.) work in some type of interactive harmony which nature seems to deem desirable, then presumably a human intervention at one or other level is capable of affecting all levels. This is not to say that religion is, or could be, a purely biochemical invention: it merely suggests that the physical and other 'non-spiritual' aspects of the human personality may also have an important role in man's spiritual and religious development.

Argyle has outlined the major psychological factors affecting religious behaviour but has only explained them in a very inadequate manner. His reliance on the traditional psychological perception of reality limits his scope of application; his focus is almost exclusively that of overt, external behaviour. Religion, on the other hand, as distinct from religious practice, is an internal, emotional, psychic primeval response to the 'life instinct', which continually projects humanity into a search for ultimate meaning, happiness and fulfilment.

The Contribution of Carl Jung

On the positive side, Carl Jung is unique for his reflection and research on the religious dimension of the human personality. Initially, a disciple of Freud, Jung parted ways with his master specifically on the issue of sexuality and aggession, which for Freud formed the all pervading forces of instinctual drives with which the super-ego and ego were in continual battle to maintain equilibrium in the human personality. For Jung, this concept of man was far too restrictive and problematic. The goal of life, Jung suggests, is the achievement of *individuation,* whereby the personality is liberated, healed and transformed through the creation of a harmonious synthesis, reconciling the functions of the collective unconscious with the demands of the conscious personality.

Freud described the unconscious as the seat of repressed, instinctual drives, revealed in dreams and resolved only in psychoanalysis. The unconscious is unique to each person. Jung, on the other hand, posited a *collective* unconscious (of which the personal unconscious is merely an expression) consisting of *archetypes:* inherited predispositions, reflecting symbolically the entire history of man. The 'Wise Old Man', 'Mother Earth', 'Rebirth', 'Trickster' are some examples of Jungian archetypes, symbolic images which signify specific qualities (e.g. wisdom, fidelity, etc.) for people in every age and culture.

Significant among these universally shared archetypal images are a set of symbols and themes which occur in every religion and mythology, ancient and modern, and are, therefore, presumed to have originated in the collective unconscious which all humans share. The vine, rock, fire, water, bread, 'innocent as a lamb', 'the wisdom of doves', 'original state of bliss', 'conceived immaculately' are among the universally shared religious archetypes. According to Jung, every religious dogma has an equivalent archetype; in fact, the influence of the unconscious on us is essentially religious in nature. Therefore, the task of religion is to give conscious expression to the archetypes, in so far as this is humanly possible. Man's psychic health and stability depend as much on the proper and appropriate expression of the religious archetypes as on the expression of the instincts. In Jungian terms we come to know God, not as a theological concept, but as a primary experience to which all theology owes it origin.

Jung attributes particular importance to religious belief in the second half of life, considering it to be particularly crucial to the maintainence of human well-being:

> Among all my patients in the second half of life – that is to say over thirty-five – there has not been one whose problem in the last resort was not that of finding a religious outlook on life. It is safe to say that everyone of them fell ill because they had lost that which the living religions of every age have given to their followers, and none of them has been really healed who did not regain his religious outlook (quoted by Roger Schmidt, pp. 228).

The formulation of religious convictions and the internalisation of these same beliefs marked not just the discovery of God but also the full experience of the archetype of the self. Religion, in the Jungian sense, seems to be the supreme norm for human wholeness and integration of personality.

Religious beliefs, Jung conceded, cannot be shown to be either true or false. Whether to believe or not is purely a matter of personal choice, governed, one presumes, by one's initial experience of religion and subsequent events of spiritual significance in one's life. Jung regarded with deep suspicion, as essentially one-sided and distorted, the rationalist tradition from which Freud and Marx judged the religious phenomenon. He was also extremely critical of the Christian Church:

> Christian civilisation has proved hollow to a terrifying degree: it is all veneer, but the inner man has remained untouched and therefore unchanged. His soul is out of key with his external beliefs. . . Too few people have experienced the divine image as the innermost possession of their own souls. Christ only meets them from without, never from within the soul; that is why dark paganism still reigns there, a paganism which, now in a form so blatant that it can no longer be denied and now in all too threadbare a disguise, is swamping the world of so-called Christian culture (*Psychology and Alchemy,* par. 12).

Jung maintains that contemporary man is as innately religious as man has been since the beginning of evolution. The abandonment of religion in western countries he would attribute, in large measure, to a failure on the part of the official churches to provide a climate conducive to the articulation of man's real spiritual needs: '. . . creed and ritual, have become so elaborated and refined that they no longer express the psychic state of the ordinary man, and religion has congealed into externals and formalities' (quoted in Frieda Fordham, p. 74).

Yet, human beings continue to be religious, even in their very denial of that fact, and the energy that formerly flowed into ritual and religious observance now find expression in political creeds, in the achievement of power, in the romanticisation of sex, or in the worship paid to new gods such as the psychologist himself/herself in modern American society.

Jung's most outstanding contribution to the study of religion is his discovery of what we may call 'inner spiritual instincts' (the religious archetypes) which always seek expression and form. If official, institutional religion fails to provide appropriate outlets for these 'instincts', then human beings will turn elsewhere and worship other Gods (albeit, false ones) in the hope of satisfying their spiritual thirst.

Religion and Humanistic Psychology

The psychology of religion is slow to adopt that Jungian position which postulates that every human being needs a God to believe-in in order to survive and, consequently, devotes a great deal of time and energy in paying homage to that God. Increasingly, psychology is acknowledging this basic premise which already has gained quite some status in the psychotherapies of those schools of psychology known as *humanistic* and *transpersonal* (otherwise called, *The Third Force*).

Humanistic psychology owes its origin to the pioneering work of Gordon Allport, Abraham Maslow, Carl Rogers, Victor Frankl, Rollo May, Erich Fromm and James Bugental. The focus in the 'Third Force' psychology is very much on creativity, cosmic awareness, self-actualisation, integration of dichotomies, transcendence, compassion, meditation and mystical fusion. Starting with human experience itself and assuming a natural, inherent potential for growth and well-being, the Third Force declares as its starting point: 'Freud supplied to us the sick half of psychology and we must now fill it out with the healthy half' (Abraham Maslow, p. 5).

The humanistic school does not deny the sinfulness or distortion of human nature, nor the human tendency to hurt and exploit; where it parts company with other schools is on the issue of instinctual drives arising from a subconscious which is considered to be a conundrum of raging uncontrolled forces, continually threatening the psychic equilibrium of man (the Freudian view). Instead, humanistic psychologists consider the human to be a creature of meaning, purpose and goal-orientated behaviour with a life-oriented behaviour arising from a deep inner core where the physical, psychic, social and spiritual dimensions are one. Distortions in human behaviour, the Third Force would claim, arise from frustrations in the human design for life caused by one's own wrong perceptions of reality or a thwarted upbringing arising from parental or environmental factors. Even where these interfere and seriously inhibit one's growth, man has an inner wisdom and will-to-meaning which enables him to cope with, and make sense out of, potentially disastrous situations.

It is sometimes alleged that humanistic psychology focuses on the individual in a narrow and self-centred way; on the contrary, it asserts quite categorically that human growth is compex and diversified and only possible in the context of relationships – with others, with nature and with the object of one's transcendence, i.e. God, by whatever name we choose to use. The human ability to transcend (the spiritual dimension) is considered to be one of the most powerfully enhancing and integrating capacities of our nature. It is not seen to be dependent on formal religion and may flourish in very powerful and life-giving ways without allegiance to any formal religious system. Although not opposed to formal religion, the Third-Force psychologists do not attribute much importance to it; some are acutely aware of the pain, guilt and useless suffering it has caused and strongly oppose the dualistic tendencies which formal religion tends to uphold:

> To the extent that this movement increasingly provides experiences of transcendence, cosmic consciousness, the Self beyond the self, or of nothingness, it may be considered religious. Although this is the direction of the movement. . . even disciplines that train for transpersonal experiences are reluctant to describe themselves as religious. The term *spiritual* has fewer establishment connotations and is more frequently used (Robert Bellah, p. 95).

Human psychology is committed to the unified growth of the human person as a body-mind-spirit continuum, with all the various components potentially geared to work for the good of the whole organism. This view of man is, in fact, identical with that envisaged by all the great mystical traditions of history and, consequently, the Third-Force psychology, by any reckoning, must be considered deeply spiritual and crucial to the development of our species in a culture growing tired of formal religion.

Precisely because of its focus on the spiritual dimension of human life and its categorical claim on the spiritual as an integral aspect of human nature, humanistic psychology has had its share of contempt and scorn. Mainstream psychology quickly dismisses its claims because there is no hard, quantitative, observable evidence to substantiate its basic tenets. Spirituality has adopted something of a 'closed-shop' mentality, claiming exclusive access to spiritual growth and accusing psychology of idolatrous claims to what is only possible purely and exclusively through the power of God. Theology, too looks somewhat askance at this movement claiming that spirituality is a divinely bestowed gift which social science can neither identify nor describe.

The opposition, especially from official churches, betrays a strong sense of threat. Triumphalistic thought-patterns still dominate religious systems, especially those which seek to evangelise and convert to 'the true way'. Although Christians acknowledge that God's coming into our world in the person and ministry of Jesus has made all things sacred (and human effort in a special way), it still refused to see and accept God at work in the 'purely secular' sphere. This apart, all the churches and all the main religions are still devilishly confused by the distinction between spirituality and religion. In so many cases the underlying assumption still seems to be: one can only be genuinely spiritual, that is, one can only respond to God's grace and call, in and through formal religious systems.

It is this very assumption that is under attack today. Anthropologically, it is no longer tenable – on the simple evidence that human beings have responded to God for some 70,000 years without any formal religion. Psychologically, the behaviouristic/mechanistic approaches fail to tap the full potential and ultimate possibilities in human feeling and motivation; in going beyond these external, observable levels, the Third-Force psychologists have probed the depths of the psyche and are helping people today to rediscover their true and *total* selves as physical-social-psychic-spiritual beings. Their success rests basically in their holistic approach as distinct from the fragmented isolated approaches of many established religions which consider the spiritual to be superior (even opposed) to the human and totally beyond the comprehension of mere human beings. For humanistic psychology there is no such thing as a 'mere human being'. Every person, it claims, is richly and diversly endowed, especially in their 'inner depths' and destined for life and meaning above and beyond the confines of the physical body.

Parapsychology, considered by some to be mere gimmickery, is also more favourably received, focusing attention on unusual powers and qualities (e.g. telepathy, clairvoyance, extra-sensory perception) which may well be common place in man's next stage of evolution.

The new threshold of man's spiritual identity, acknowledged by anthropology and psychology has also become an important point of interest for physics and biology (see chapter 8). All branches of contemporary science, having exhausted the so-called scientific method and now striving to outgrow its limitations, are in the process of creating new horizons. The focus is on possibilities rather than probabilities, horizons rather than limitations, dreams rather than proofs, open systems rather than closed ones. In this way the intangibles of human nature, such as beauty, harmony and godliness become the core elements in the science of tomorrow. In fact, it is only by incorporating these illusive elments that modern science can survive and thus respond to the needs of the total person approaching a new threshold of evolutionary growth.

Protagonists of the holistic concept of life and well-being are prophets of our time. Like all prophets, they will be rejected, rebuffed and perhaps driven underground by the official establishments, including the religious ones. Nonetheless, their spirit will survive and ultimately triumph. And in the transformation from one quality of culture to another there will inevitably be mishaps and growing pains of change.

It is true that many people today are discovering God in social science rather than in official religion and who are we to say that God cannot reveal himself through psychology or anthropology, especially if his Spirit becomes choked and stifled in the trimmings of official religion. It is valid to assert that the God of psychology, of TM or of Marxism is a false God who will not ultimately satisfy the needs and aspirations of the human heart. However, the searcher who latches on to the 'false God' is often pursuing a more authentic spiritual journey than the orthodox believer who has never ventured out from beneath the canopy of truth as upheld by official religion; in time, that searcher stands a good chance of finding the true God, the God of all peoples.

Stages of Faith Development

Throughout the 1970s a good deal of attention was given to the stage of faith development in human beings, that process of growth whereby people come to an awareness and ownership of their belief. James W. Fowler's work is perhaps the best known:

> I believe faith is a human universal. We are endowed at birth with nascent capacities for faith. How these capacities are activated and grow depends to a large extent on how we are welcomed into the world and

what kind of environment we grow in. Faith is interactive and social; it requires community, language, ritual and nurture. Faith is also shaped by initiatives of spirit and grace. How these latter initiatives are recognised and imaged or unperceived and ignored, powerfully affect the shape of faith in our lives (Fowler, p. xiii).

Fowler bases his assumptions on the combined developmental theories of Lawrence Kohlberg, E. H. Erikson and Daniel J. Levinson and outlines seven stages of faith development corresponding to the various stages of psychosocial growth as outlined by developmental psychology (see diagram). Fowler's seven stages while incapable of being clearly differentiated, are a useful working model and enlighten our understanding of faith development in human beings. Worthy of special note is Fowler's description of the young adult phase wherein the first ownership of one's faith takes place, a stage of spiritual development we normally expect from our

Stages of Personal/Faith Development

Stage	Personal	Religious	Moral
Infancy (0–1½)	Trust v. Mistrust	Undifferentiated Faith	
			Preconvential
Early Childhood (2–6)	Autonomy v. Shame Initiative v. Guilt	Intuitive–Projective Faith	Instrumental Exchange
Childhood (7–12)	Industry v. Inferiority	Mythic v. Literal Faith	
Adolescence (13–21)	Identity v. Role Confusion	Synthetic– Conventional Faith	*Conventional* Mutual, Inter- personal relations
Young Adult (21–35)	Intimacy v. Isolation	Individuative– Reflective Faith	Social System and Conscience
Adulthood (35–60)	Generativity v. Stagnation	Conjunctive Faith	Social Contract Individual Rights
Maturity (60–)	Integrity v. Despair	Universalising Faith	Universal, ethical principles
	Source: Erik Erikson & D. J. Levinson	*Source:* James Fowler, Sam Keen & Others	*Source:* Lawrence Kohlberg

adolescents, especially in terms of compliance with religious rules and ritual. Fowler even goes further and suggests that the real ownership of one's faith may not take place until after a successful resolution of the mid-life transition, sometime between the ages of forty and fifty.

In psychological terms, 'faith is a generic feature of the human struggle to find and maintain meaning and it may or may not find religious expression (Fowler, p. 91). It is a life-long process, enhanced and, perhaps, also hindered by parental and societal models, growing through uncertainty, doubt, questioning, reflection, articulation and ownership of one's convictions, over a long number of years. In this life, faith is never finally discovered. It involves a continual struggle and search, a growing and deepening. Thus each new stage means:

— a new depth of understanding at the intellectual, emotional and spiritual levels;
— an augmented capacity to perceive the belief system of another and integrate it with one's own spiritual vision;
— as in Kohlberg's theory, an increased sense of morality;
— a more self-reliant and increasingly objective accounting for the warrants and justifications of one's faith and for the personal commitment involved in same;
— a readiness to take responsibility for the quality of faith expression through appropriate symbols, stories and ritual;
— an increased commitment to the communal nature of faith, to the common task of creating the unity and coherence of one's meaningful world.

Humanistic psychology, in agreement with other major schools, acknowledges that religion can become a crutch to lean on and a mechanism to escape from the challenges of life, but accuses these other approaches of creating a self-fulfilling prophesy: if one postulates that man is a victim of unconscious drives (Freudian theory) or a mere mechanistic 'animal' (Behaviourism), then one has closed all possibilities of perceiving the full and total person. Instead, the Third-Force suggests that we perceive in a non-judgemental way the human person in the totality of life and action, individually and communally (hence, the Rogerian emphasis on the encounter group), societally and globally. We adopt an attitude of listening, of being open and receptive to the diversity of human experience and aspiration, and that we strive to decipher the underlying dynamics that make man a *homo poeta,* 'man the meaning-maker'. From this breadth of vision and perspective the humanistic psychologist is not particularly interested in religion or faith as an object in its own right, but as a dimension of human life, touching every aspect of our humanity (health, material values, societal norms, social expectations, etc.) and inherent in every human aspiration.

Although he has not been classified as a humanistic psychologist, Fowler is in close sympathy with these trends and his response to the critics who say he is cheapening faith and making it far too ungodlike would be representative of the Third-Force position:

> Wherever I lecture or speak about faith development research I meet people who suggest that I should choose some other term to describe the focus of this work. . . Several groups of critics have a deep suspicion that adolescents, especially in terms of compliance with religious rule the concept of faith is really inseparable from religion and belief. . . They reject the claim that faith is a generic feature of the human struggle to find and maintain meaning and that it may or may not find religious expression. Their proposed substitutions for faith go in two directions. Those who are favourable to religion and would like to see this kind of work fully identified with the scientific study of religion feel that I would be more honest if I simply described it as research on religious development. On the other hand, persons who fear that the linkage of faith and religion taints or limits the usefulness of an otherwise promising body of theory urge that I take the opposite direction. They suggest the use of some more strictly secular term. . 'world view development', 'belief system formation', 'development of consciousness', as categories that would help avoid confusion (Fowler, p. 91).

No statement so cryptically captivates the common and popular perception of faith and religion as synonymous entities along with the still prevalent conviction that faith is some type of super-mundane, super-human phenomenon that humans should not analyse or investigate. In large measure the official churches must hold responsibility for their disembodied, restrictive and stifling notion of man's spiritual capacity. The church and its theologians run a continued risk of such restrictive thinking until they begin a more open dialogue with the social sciences and acknowledge their invaluable insights into the growth and development of the total person.

Bibliography

Argyle, M., 'Seven Psychological Roots of Religion', *Theology*, 67 (1964), pp. 1-7.

Bellah, Robert (ed.), *The New Religious Consciousness,* University of California Press, 1976.

Feuerbach, Ludwig, *The Essence of Christianity,* New York: Harper, 1957.

Fordham, Frieda, *An Introduction to Jung's Psychology,* Penguin, 1953.

Fowler, James W. *Stages of Faith,* Harper & Row, 1981.

Freud, Sigmund, *The Future of an Illusion,* London: Leonard & Virginia Woolf, 1928 (Vol. 21 of the Strachey edition of Freud's published works).

Heisig, J. W. *Imago Dei: A Study of C. G. Jung's Psychology of Religion,* London: Associated University Presses, 1979.

Jung, C. G. *The Structure and Dynamics of the Psyche; Civilisation in Transition; Psychology and Religion: West and East; Psychology and Alchemy;* vols. 8, 10, 11, 12 respectively of *The Collected Works of Carl Jung,* edited by Gerhard Adler, Michael Fordham & Herbert Read, published in London by Routledge and Kegan Paul and in New York by the Bollington Foundation (distributed by Pantheon Books).

Marx, Karl, *Early Writings,* McGraw-Hill, 1963.

Maslow, Abraham, *Towards a Psychology of Being,* Van Nostrand Reinhold, 1962.

Schmidt, Roger, *Exploring Religion,* California,: Wadsworth, 1980.

4

Sacred Dance and Ritual Play
(Celebration)

The sacred traditions of the world are an abundant repository of man's symbols as metaphors of mystery.
— MARIA-GABRIELE WOSIEN

In all the wild imaginings of mythology a fanciful spirit is playing on the borderline between jest and earnest. — J. HUIZINGA

Meaning is not in things, but in between. — NORMAN O. BROWN

JOHAN HUIZINGA coined the term *Homo Ludens* to describe one of the most intricate and fascinating dimensions of human evolution, the capacity for fun, jest, frivolity, laughter — that entire repertoire of behaviour pertaining either to the escape from seriousness or the transformation of the serious. Huizinga went so far as to suggest that play is the basis of culture and that historical cultural activities such as law, war, education, poetry, philosophy and art are the stylised and formalised expressions of what was initially a primitive, agonistic, heroic urge. For Huizinga, play is the most powerful metaphor available to explain serious cultural meaning.

David L. Miller and Norman O. Brown both explore Huizinga's insight in greater depth. Miller's conviction that the mythological, the aesthetic and the mysterious, which together form the inner core of all genuine religion, can only be expressed and thus experienced in a playful way, is basic to any thorough understanding of man and his religion.

The sociology and psychology of play highlight the human and social need to 'let go' and experience those other feelings of our being which are suspended in more rational and serious behaviour. The study of human playfulness in an evolutionary (anthropological) context shows it to be a core element which is powerfully integrated with every dimension of primitive behaviour. 'By considering the whole sphere of so-called primitive culture as a play-sphere,' says Huizinga, '. . . we pave the way for a more direct and general understanding of its peculiarities than any meticulous psychological or sociological analysis would allow.' (Huizinga, p. 25)

Primitive religion is very much an experience of playfulness, albeit, a serious playfulness. Like its mythological parent it arose from the unfolding story of human evolution recording the human endeavour to find one's true place in the universe. Primitive mythology created the story and provided the symbols through which the story could be expressed in appropriate ritual. Enacting the ritual and relating it to the experience of life became the formal function of religion. The range of religious expression, the creation of religious ritual, arose entirely from the human psyche. There were no divine precedents nor revelations; such disclosures would, in fact, contravene the creativity and spontaneity of the Spirit arising from within the sacredness of humanity itself.

The Sacred Dance

One does not wish to suggest that primitive forms of religious expression (and experience) were above defect. Compared with contemporary religious ritual they embodied a great deal of spontaneity and immediacy which gave them an ecstatic and transforming power, far exceeding that experienced in religion today; ancient forms also possessed an unique capacity to satisfy spiritual hunger and raise the level of creative consciousness. Foremost among primitive rituals is the *Sacred Dance* which, according to Wach (p. 106) is still found among primitive tribes in Australia, Polynesia, Africa, south-eastern Asia, northern Asia, the Near and Far East.

Wosien's description of the Sacred Dance is worth quoting at some length:

> Dance, as an expression of man being moved by the transcendent power, is also the earliest art form; before man expresses his experience of life through materials, he does so with his body. Early man dances on every occasion; for joy, grief, love, fear, at sunrise, death, birth. The movement of the dance provides him with a deepening of his experience. . . In whatever form the dance presents itself, it always aims at approaching the God. . .

All dance, being imitative, aims at achieving identity with the thing observed and danced out. It is and gives ecstasy by virtue of being in touch with the life-force. The mind is in the twilight state beyond thinking and willing where something else moves it, just as we, in our best moments, have the feeling of being lived by Life.

The sacred dance traditions of the world show a truly amazing abundance of imagined forms through which men, everywhere, have sought to relate themselves to the wonder of existence. Its heritage is a reflection of the never-ending play of Life with its own created forms. By acting out his inner experiences man gains clarity about the nature of the images generated in his own psyche, through which he is able to relate to outward creation. In this way, external actions and inner experience cannot be separated, because the essence of both is wholeness and integration (Wosien, pp. 8-9, 11-12).

According to R. R. Marett (pp. 175, 180) the savage does not preach his religion but dances it instead. In this ritualistic behaviour the individual transcends himself. He dances in order to overcome the empirical self, to connect with his inner spirit and enjoy the integrated experience of being one's true self. In this mystic or ecstatic moment the dancer is elevated into a new awareness. He transcends the greyness and ambiguity of daily life and enters a new realm of being where he really feels at home.

It would be wrong to suggest that this deeply personal experience allures the dancer from the 'real' world and wraps him in a false world of selfish ecstasy. As Wach points out, the sacred dance has social, indeed, global dimensions: 'It is the affirmation of the cohesion of the group in its communion with nature, with the ancestors, with the source of life.' (p. 137) In fact, it is meaningless outside the group context, or what we might call 'the worshipping community'. The dancer experiences a new sense of identity within the group and affirms the group in its experience of transcending. At a more mysterious level it connects individual and group with the Great Cosmic Dance, an intense emotional and spiritual experience which was probably something akin to that state of being experienced by Peter on the mountain of the transfiguration when he said; 'Lord, it is good for us to be here' (Mk 9:5).

Eastern religions with their more intuitive perception of reality have retained semblances of the sacred dance in a much more explicit way than the dominant religions of the west. In India there are four classical schools of dance, all with distinctive religious (Hindu) connotations: (a) *Bharata Natyam*, performed mainly by the female temple dancers of south India, quite austere in form, although, today, not as explicitly religious as it used to be; (b) *Kathanali*, a south Indian male dance based on the great Hindu epics; (c) *Kathak*, once performed by priests only, used today to entertain the Muslim and Hindu courts of North India by relating the erotic exploits of the God, Krishna; (d) the graceful, restful *manipuri* of north-eastern India in which court ladies depict legends of Krishna. According to the theory of Tantric (Magical) Buddhism, a valid ritual action must involve all three sides of our being; body, speech and mind; dance serves as the most potent expression of body language. Forms of dance are also known in the monasteries of the Lama tradition and in certain shamanistic rites of Tibet. In Islam, the dancing dervishes continue an age-old form of ecstatic dance. The dancing customs of contemporary tribal peoples, such as the Indian sundown dance, are quite well known and all these have distinctive religious symbolism.

What one says of the sacred dance can be applied to any form of dance, ancient or contemporary. That is not to say that the so-called sacred dance was in fact something quite secular. Every form of dance is in some sense sacred. People of all ages and cultures love dancing, except those who have lost touch with the 'child' within themselves. Dancing is not something we learn, it comes naturally. Even when specific patterns are being taught, they are usually attained with great facility.

Modern forms of popular dance, such as jazz, rock and roll, punk-dance, etc., evoke very deep and powerful sentiments in the dancer, and notably for a younger, atheistic generation. A little imagination is enough to note the obvious: devoid of a God-experience in the official, cultural channels, modern youth seek it (and find it) in their dance and music. Modern music festivals, it is well known, are also accompanied by a great deal of sexual and drug-related exploration, two of the other leading 'gods' of the contemporary world. Our young people may not be able to name their god – the very word switches them off – nor recognise the inner tendency to transcend and give expression to our spiritual selves, but they do worship a deity, frequently amid the deafening noise of a modern disco.

The sacred dance is not just a feature of pre-logical man, or a fascinating custom of contemporary illiterate societies; it is a permanent feature of human nature and touches the very core of our spiritual identity. Religion, if real and authentic, is an experience of celebration, of playfulness, of letting-go, of transcending the mundane and rational, of reaching the divine, both within and without.

The recent upsurge of the charismatic renewal movement in the Catholic Church and of the pentecostal movement in other Christian faiths, is also an effort to recapture the spontaneity and joy of our spiritual selves. Speaking in tongues, clapping hands, singing aloud, dancing for joy, are supra-rational modes of expression for a true inner experience of that which cannot be rationally articulated. That such movements often attract emotionally unbalanced people may be, in fact, a mark of their authenticity.

The Playfulness of Primitive Cult

On does not wish to suggest that the sacred dance is the kernal of primitive religion. It is only one expression of a culture for which creative action was more important than the most seminal ideas:

> Primitive reality is above all a world of behaviour, a world in which everything is seen as gesture, as it were – physiognomically – and where everything either personal or thing-like exists in action. It is not a world of knowledge but one of deed; it is not static, but dynamic; not theoretical but pragmatic (Heinz Werner, p. 402).

Anthropologically, religion-in-action is known as *cult*, and the nature of primitive cult is best gleaned from contemporary customs of tribal people in Africa and Asia. Ceremonies tend to be very colourful, highly ritualistic and exuberant in joy and song. Symbolism tends to be intricate and often a carefully preserved secret of the tribe itself, whose members participate in the ritual with great willingness, enthusiasm and usually in very big numbers.

Various expressions of ancient worship outlined in chapter 1 tell us something of the primitive sense of religious celebration. Best known among these is *magic*. Drawing on Freudian and Piagetian insights on childhood perception, Campbell suggests that the use of magic implies a certain world view, or perception of reality, common to primitive people and not altogether absent in the world of our own time:

> The child's world is alert and alive governed by rules of response and command, not by physical laws; a portentous continuum of consciousness, endowed with purpose and intent, either resistent or responsive to the child itself. As we know, this infantile notion (or something much

like it) of a world (is) governed rather by a superordinated parental personality instead of impersonal physical forces, and oriented to the weal and woe of man. . . (Campbell, p. 81)

Magic rituals tend to be very elaborate, solemn and serious. A great deal of primitive magic centres on the control and manipulation of natural forces. Primitive man was keenly conscious of his dependence on nature, his interaction with it and its potential benefits for his happiness and well-being. Contrary to modern technology, which also seeks to conquer and manipulate natural forces, ancient man never entertained the idea of a direct intervention in nature. Instead, magic recognises the ultimate, supernatural control of creation and seeks to influence the supernatural by the petitionary ritual behaviour inherent in the magical rite. Indirectly, then, magic is a celebration of life, of man's power to influence and change life, but also an acknowledgement of man's ultimate and total dependence on forces outside and beyond himself, his dependence on which is somehow transcended in the magical act. At every level, magic proclaims a triumph for man and hence its widespread use in ancient belief systems and in tribal religions to our own day.

The role of witchcraft, still widely practiced in parts of Africa, is akin to that of magic, except here the focus tends to be on health and personal well-being. Medicine and religion have, until recent times, been closely aligned in human development. The well-being of the soul, the health of the body and the happiness of the person were considered in unison until Greek philosophy with its passion for clearcut distinctions and dualistic opposition created artificial dividing lines which have dominated our western value-system to the present day.

The integration of physical and spiritual health in ancient times is well portrayed in the person of the *shaman*, one endowed with ecstatic power, with special access to the supernatural. He absorbs and communicates a special mode of sustaining and healing power. The shaman was particularly associated with trance states, capable of manipulating consciousness. His lifestyle has parallels in the monastic system of all major religions: one of renunciation and simplicity, long periods of solitude and the ability to perform miraculous events, especially, healing. Unlike the contemporary monk, the shaman was integrally a part of society, called upon for help in any human predicament. Even in the hunting customs of early man, the blessing and advice of the shaman was frequently invoked.

The shaman stood between the gods and the people, representing the mystery of divinity in his altered state of consciousness and the goodness of God in aiding the people. The shaman became a key figure in the celebration of life, embodying in himself the distance and nearness of God and also the potential and predicament of man.

Finally, a word about totemic rites. No other form of ancient ritual seems to have had such power of cohesion and fellowship as the celebration of totemism. According to this custom, members of a clan considered themselves to be in kinship (fellowship) with a specific plant or animal, from whom they assumed a common descendancy, one who represents for them a supernatural power on which they have special claim. Arising from the common allegiance to the totem plant or animal, is a specific set of social regulations governing the life of the group; these regulations usually included the non-destruction of the species of plant or animal associated with the totem. Once again, we see the ancient respect for life-forms, natural and human alike. For the clan, a key moment of unity and celebration was the ritual consuming of the totem animal's blood. Here, as in other forms of ancient worship, we see a prototype of the Christian concept of sacrament.

In tribal societies 'sacramental' or cultic action is occasioned by important events in the lives of individuals, in the life of the tribe or in the cycle of the seasons. Of particular significance are *initiation rites*, introducing the neophyte into the clan, into adolescence, into betrothal or marriage. Mircea Eliade suggests that initiation rites have an unique place in religion (and always have had) because they pertain to origins, the fundamental, philosophical questions ('where did we come from', 'where did it all begin', etc.), which have been foremost in the human mind for millions of years. The symbolic impact of initiation ceremonies is much richer and consequently has a far greater facility to confer meaning in tribal religions than in contemporary formal ones.

The Catholic sacrament of Confirmation, intended to symbolise and celebrate the transition into adulthood, has lost virtually all semblance of an initiation rite. The fact that the sacraments of the Christian churches and sacred ceremonies of other faiths have become criteria for moral rectitude and indicators of affiliation to one or other church marks a tragic departure from their real meaning. The fact that many of our symbol-systems in contemporary religion no longer function symbolically, negates not merely the meaning of the rites, but the fundamental coherence-for-life which such rites alone can confer. When symbolism becomes outdated or routinised in monotonously repeated rituals, then it no longer serves the transformation of the human spirit, the ability to transcend and, hence, stifles the true joy and celebration of life.

Celebrating the Serious Side of Life

In ritual terms, the word *celebration* has a rich connotation and may not always imply joy or laughter. Concern for the dead, the impending awareness that they were somehow still alive, understood in terms of reincarnation or otherwise, seems to have led to some of the earliest formulations of ritual ceremony. We have anthropological evidence to suggest that ritual burials date back some 60,000 years ago. Yet, this concern with death and after-life had a remarkable, positive vision, considering the precarious nature of life at that time. An awareness of after-life and of the power of the dead to influence events and circumstances for the living, seems to be a feature of early human consciousness. Consequently, burial rites, while being a form of mourning, seem to be primarily designed to celebrate the on-going life, the reincarnation, the cyclic nature by which the human spirit survived.

Ancestral worship also had a remarkable affinity with nature, arising from a total human dependence on the produce of the earth and the benigness of nature for survival and growth. Seasonal fluctuations, weather variations, storms and other major disruptions in the natural process, all became the objects of ritual ceremony. The dominant mood was not so much fear as wonder. Through the ritualistic process, our ancestors sought to understand and comprehend the awesome and mysterious power beyond, an influence they considered primarily benign and hence their efforts to influence it to their advantage through magic, shamanistic rites and other ritual practices. Once again, we detect an amazing faith in the goodness of providence, even in the face of tragedy and disaster.

This affective respect for the created order permeated even their crude skills of food provision. Hunting and killing their prey was not nearly as rampant and indiscriminate as is frequently suggested. Hunting-man was not the starved, reckless savage so frequently portrayed. Increasingly, anthropological evidence suggests that hunting practices were often highly ritualised. Joseph Campbell (pp. 282-289) quotes a classic example of the hunting and killing of a large number of buffalo as followed today by the Blackfoot Indians of Montana and also practised in Europe, he claims, between 30,000 and 10,000 BC. The buffalo are lured by masked shamans into a grand buffalo dance (note the parallel with the sacred dance), eventually leading the flock to the verge of a cliff where they fall over and are killed. The dance, however, is no mere empty ritual; it is a magical rite which is understood to guarantee the survival of the 'inner' life. Campbell explains it thus:

> For where there is magic there is no death. And where the animal rites are properly celebrated by the people, there is a magical, wonderful accord between the beasts and those who have to hunt them. The buffalo dance, properly performed, insures that the creatures slaughtered shall be giving only their bodies, not their essence, not their lives. And so they will live again, or rather, live on, and will be there to return the following season. The hunt itself, therefore, is a rite of sacrifice, sacred, and not a rawly secular affair.

The concept of sacrifice in every living religion arises from primitive custom, where it has a rich and complex meaning, centred on the sacredness of all individual life-forms and the intimate interdependence that existed between these forms, whether plant, animal, human, super-human. Our ancient ancestors, the so-called aggressive predators, possessed an acute, ecological consciousness which recent research is slowly unravelling. From this deep respect for nature and the supernatural, both within and outside their world, the primitives developed their patterns of ritual, the prototype of all religious ceremony in our world today.

The Decline of Ritual

Ritual like religion itself is a product of time and place. It arises from a fundamental myth which seeks to articulate the dream or vision of life inherent in the contemporary culture. The myth projects itself in symbol and necessitates symbolic expression which we encounter in ritual, rite and ceremony. Without myth, symbol and ritual, life is fragmented and disorientated, devoid of meaning and, consequently, existence becomes morbid for the average human being. Man, however, will not accept this ambiguity for long. Order, purpose, direction and meaning are among the primary ingredients of human existence. If they cease to be made available through the official channels of church or state, human beings will create them for themselves. Moreover, they will *recreate* them in socially accepted modes of behaviour.

Today, human culture is in a shambles. We live in what Roszak appropriately calls a *wasteland,* one of confused values, fragmented relationships, alienated human beings, a polluted earth. Our glorious heritage of myth, symbol, ritual and religion unravelled over thousands of years (perhaps 600,000 years in all) in gentle and painstaking fashion is today choked, stifled and usurped in systems and institutions designed to serve a contemporary human being who is obsessed by structures and stability because he has lost his eclectic bearings with the breadth and depth of life.

The contemporary automan, the product of high and hard technology, is desperately out of tune with the rhythm of life. We find him (and let us note it is *him* rather than *her*) at all the control points of contemporary institutions in both church and state, immersed in a battle for power, which runs the risk of destroying our entire universe. Experientially, our automan lives in a void, where feelings are camouflaged, distorted and dissipated amid the cheap thrills of drugs, sex, pleasure, prestige and power, the contrived myths of our age. Precisely because we live in such a contrived state, 'the celebration of life' has become an enigma, not least in the lifeless, liturgical rituals of our religious systems.

Following the cycle of Life-Death-Resurrection, outlined in chapter 6, we know this process has a limited time-scale. As the crisis deepens the moment of truth approaches and increasingly the dawn of the twenty-first century seems to be the moment of new hope. A counter-culture, incorporating new human, ecological and spiritual values is slowly and gently arising in the northern hemisphere. A new global consciousness is being forged by the east-west dialogue. The breakdown of western society is but the Calvary before the Resurrection.

Features of Homo Religiosus

A first sign of the new era is a return to our own *centre*, individually and as a species. What is the experience of being human on this earth in fellowship with all other life-forms? In responding to this question, we experience the naked truth of our own existence. As people respond to this question, as they connect with their own in-depth experience (with the *God-within*), they come to a perception of life remarkably similar to the main features of religious experience outlined by Wach (pp. 30ff) in his study of *Homo Religiosus*:

1. *Ultimacy*: My experience of life leads me to posit 'a beyond', by whatever name I call it, that affects and touches the reality of my experience, which some people describe as that which gives 'heart' to their daily existence.

2. *Encounter*: I experience an urge to say 'Yes' to an invitation, perhaps, often expressed in the ambiguity of Pascal's perception that he would not be seeking God only that God had already found him. Many philosophers and spiritual writers refer to this 'dark night' experience.

3. *Dynamism*: A genuinely spiritual experience is never static, complete, totally comprehensible; it is a *process* rather than a *product*.

4. *Personal*: The total person, and not just the intellect or will (to which traditional western philosophy has given undue attention), responds to the invitation to ultimate meaning. Genuine spirituality has to do primarily with the *heart* (as the seat of emotion and feeling) and not with the *head*.

5. *Intensity*: 'Potentially,' says Wach, (p. 35) 'this is the most powerful, comprehensive, shattering and profound experience of which man is capable.' It touches the core of one's being in a way that commands allegiance, eliciting a response which rules or moral obligations can never hope to generate.

Official religion claims that such experience is the special privilege of the chosen few. With Wach, I would like to suggest that this experience is within reach of every human being as something that arises from within our humanity and is potentially capable of being nurtured by the rhythm of life itself. The universal nature of such experience is outlined by Wach (pp. 38-39) in a passage where he draws on a wide variety of informed opinion:

> Genuine religious experience . . . is universal. The anthropologists, such as Marett and Malinowski, have proved that, far from being artificially induced ('invented' as the age of enlightenment believed it to be), religion

is an ubiquitous expression of the *sensus numinis* (Otto's now famous term). Henri Bergson has stated: 'There has never been a society without religion,' and Raymond Firth confirms that 'Religion is universal in human societies.' It was Marett who suggested that we might change the title *Homo Sapiens* into *Homo Religiosus*. As the modern anthropologist, Evans-Pritchard, very well puts it: 'If we are attempting to understand Islam . . . or Christianity or Hinduism, it is a great help toward our understanding of it if we know that certain features of it are universal, features of all religions, including those of the most primitive peoples; yet others are features of certain types of religion; and yet others are distincitve of that religion alone.' Robert Redfield enumerates the following as 'universal features': recognition of the self and others, groupings of people, ways of confronting the inevitable experiences of the human career, confrontation of Not-Me (including earth, sky, night, and 'invisible beings, wills and powers') in some ordered relationship. There is a disposition, a propensity – a nisus – in man to worship and to respond to divine self-disclosure. As Webb has aptly expressed it: 'thus I would see in the religious experience of mankind as a whole, a genuine unity and would consider it as the response of the human spirit to the Divine Spirit with which it is by the necessity, of its nature in propositional contact.'

Religious systems today are so fossilised and fabricated that they fail to awaken genuinely numinous experiences. They do not lead to the real God but to fabricated ones, idolatrous images created by man to fulfil gross needs, based on selfish advancement. We continue to create the religion we live by and the quality of that creation depends on the quality of our perception, in other words, the level of our consciousness. Our vision of life today, especially in the northern hemisphere, is predominantly a pleasure-seeking one and as Freud so perceptively diagnosed some fifty years ago, when pleasure becomes an end in itself (i.e. a major pre-occupation) it becomes a powerfully destructive force (cf. *Beyond the Pleasure Principle*).

The gods of contemporary religion serve well our functional, utilitarian, pleasure-oriented society, and our urge to manipulate life has become so sinister and autocratic that we simply drop those gods if we feel they no longer suit us. Our culture is essentially a death-culture, marked by crime, vandalism, abortion, warfare and the more subtle destructiveness of spirit in the alienation and meaninglessness of modern life. In such an environment, the celebration of life becomes painfully paradoxical and this resonates in the quality and tone of our liturgies, parties and other celebratory functions. Celebrating a marriage ceremony, religiously and secularly, can be quite ambiguous in a society where the institution of marriage has become trivialised and problematic.

There certainly is a need for change, and while many acknowledge this few seem to have either the conviction, vision, or energy to bring it about. Some awareness of our evolutionary heritage, as outlined in this chapter, may serve to animate, motivate and move us towards appropriate action. The greatest transformation, however, has to be a self-transformation, from our grossly mechanistic perception of life to a more holistic one, wherein the total spectrum of life, including the spiritual, becomes the target for our new vision, and this presupposes a re-education of the masses which is a daunting challenge.

There is, however, a final ray of hope: the momentum inherent in the evolutionary process itself which has traversed its course without man for 99% of the evolutionary time-scale, and presumably will continue to do so even if interrupted by a nuclear holocaust. Teilhard de Chardin, some forty years ago, claimed that man's physical evolution was virtually complete and a new evolutionary threshold, that of *mind*, had been reached. The spontaneous orientation from the mechanistic view of life to the holistic one – with the emphasis on the mental, psychic and spiritual development seems to verify de Chardin's perception. Our new global consciousness, instigated in large measure by the wisdom from the east, marks another new departure with major repercussions for the future of mankind.

And from within this new vision, *Homo Religiosus* seems set on a new course, groping through the web of idolatrous distortions to the true God of all peoples. When this God is encountered in the human heart and at the heart of the world then the celebration of life and the celebration of religion become one and the same reality. It is a hope-filled future, but it is we ourselves and not the gods we worship, who will make it a dream come true.

Bibliography

Brown, Norman O., *Love's Body*, Random House, 1966.

Campbell, Joseph, *The Masks of God: Primitive Mythology*, The Viking Press, 1959.

Clarke, R. & Hendley, G., *The Challenge of the Primitives*, London: Cape, 1975.

Freud, Sigmund, *Beyond the Pleasure Principle* in *The Complete Psychological Works of Sigmund Freud*, vol. 18, edited by James Strachey and published by the Hogarth Press, London, 1955.

Huizinga, Johan, *Homo Ludens: a Study of the Play Element in Culture*, Beacon Press, 1950.

Leakey Richard, *The Making of Mankind*, E. P. Dutton, 1981.

Marett, R.R., *Threshold of Religion*, Methuen, 1914.

Miller, David L., *Gods and Games; Towards a Theology of Play*, Harper & Row, 1970.

Roszak, Theodore, *Where the Wasteland Ends*, London: Faber, 1973.

Wach, Joachim, *The Comparative Study of Religion*, Columbia University Press, 1958.

Werner, Heinz, *Comparative Psychology of Mental Development*, Faber, 1951.

Wosien, Maria-Gabriele, *Sacred Dance: Encounter With the Gods*, London: Thames & Hudson, 1974.

5

Cherishing Our Sacred Space
(Ecology)

Heaven was invented to satisfy those human beings to whom the earth offers nothing. — HEINE (friend of Karl Marx)

Remain faithful to the earth; but the earth has no other refuge except to become invisible: in us. — NORMAN O. BROWN

There are no redeemed enclaves within an unredeemed world.
— WALBERT BUHLMANN

ECOLOGY has been defined as the study of the inter-relationship of bodies in community, with systems of energy flow, their interdependence and their transformations. It is not concerned with entities but with the creative interaction of all life-forms ranging from individuals to populations to communities to ecosystems and finally, to the biosphere itself. Faced with the contemporary desecration of many life-forms, the brutal and selfish exploitation of natural resources, mass pollution and, not least, the human potential to destroy all life on this earth, ecology is emerging as one of the most prophetic and urgent enterprises of our age.

Religious Attitudes to the Earth

Modern religion has never quite acknowledged its affiliation with ecology, and theological reflection of the present century has done relatively little to complement other scientific reflection on ecological issues. Most modern religious systems tend to look askance, if not suspiciously, at the earth and its life-forms, often viewing these as somehow opposed and, perhaps, alien to the higher, more sublime, spiritual life-forms. The Judaeo-Christian disdain for material and created things is frequently quoted and blamed for Christianity's continuing distance from created and earthly life. In fact, Christianity tends to be quite positive about secular reality and throughout the 1960s and 1970s made many valiant efforts to re-interpret and re-express Christianity's love for creation and its eagerness to express in today's language God's revelation to human beings at the heart of the world, immersed in the God-given task of furthering human and material growth.

Even in the early church, when the 'life of perfection' was identified with 'abandoning the world', such withdrawal was always considered temporary. The recluse came back purified and radiant with the goodness of God for the benefit of his fellow men and women (e.g. St Anthony of Egypt). The anti-world stance which we wrongly attribute to early Christianity is, in fact, much more the product of post-Reformation times, when the Catholic Church in particular perceived itself as the depository of pure Christianity and sought to innoculate and shelter all its members against the heretical influences of the secular world.

All the major religions, at some point of their development, have exhibited anti-mundane traits, quite contrary to their basic philosophy of man and creation. As a general rule one can say that the more religion becomes enmeshed in its own preservation and survival, the more it deviates from its service of people (and the world) without whom its existence is irrelevant anyhow. The more it encounters mankind and the world, the more it is capable of being a leaven, enlivening and enriching the quality of life, both human and earthly. Religion was never destined to be a body of sacred theory; its context, the only situation where it makes sense, is in the life of people as they interact with each other and with the earth we all inhabit. Religion arises from within creation and therein alone can it find appropriate expression; *it is innately ecological.*

Much could be said about the contemporary relationship of religion and secularity, and the widespread desire for greater synchrony between ecology and religion. Once again, the contemporary debate can be grossly misleading and project an alleged historical image, which, in fact, belongs only to a minute moment of time. The human story as it unfolds in earliest times is very much one of man at home in the universe, in tune with nature, frightened by its threats, marvelling at its wonders and always grateful for its support and sustenance.

Ecology in Primitive Religion

Man's earliest religious aspirations find earthly and secular expression. Apart from worshipping the sun, moon and stars, human beings experienced the angry God in the storms and disasters of nature and communicated with the loving, nurturing God in the flow of the seasons and the produce of the earth. They experienced the closeness of God by worshipping objects of the earth and many of the cave drawings of Upper Paleolithic times reveal an awareness of God in and through animals and other living species of the time.

In this close harmony with nature our ancestors lived for at least two million years (since *Homo Erectus* emerged). In fact, the first serious departure from our natural habitat only came about with the industrial revolution of the late nineteenth and early twentieth centuries, and already within one-hundred years, there is an accelerating awareness of our gross abuse of the natural process and of the need to return to a more loving, caring and respectful interaction with mother earth.

Modern ecology has initiated a new dialogue with the earth and its life-force. It seeks a rebalance of care and consideration, gentleness and interdependence. It then goes on to outline broad, working principles which fascinate the anthropologist because they largely articulate the religious aspirations of our primitive ancestors at a time when religion and ecology were virtually synonymous. For our ancestors and for modern ecology, all life-forms spring from the common origin of nature. All creatures, including man, evolved from nature and by living in harmony with nature, humans discovered their best opportunities for creativity, rest and recreation.

Primitive man in his imaginative and emotional capacities, was not a passive observer of the earth and its processes. The fact that our prehistoric ancestors spent their daily lives in close contact with nature, for thousands of years, made possible an understanding of the natural world, not available to many people in our so-called developed age.

In prehistoric times the earth was not perceived as an *object*, but rather as a *subject*, a 'living' organism, awesome and threatening, but for the greater part, benevolent to humanity. Humans felt bonded with the earth in a relationship akin to that of mother and child. Thus, there arose a spirituality of the earth, a mysticism of creation, which recurs in the mystical traditions of all the major religions: man *is* the earth and in humanity the earth finds new expression as a living, feeling, conscious organism. Over the past ten years both science and spirituality have rediscovered the sacredness of nature, forging yet another link with the faith we have inherited from of old (cf. Matthew Fox).

Civilisation, too, is rooted in nature; nature has shaped human culture and influences all artistic and scientific achievement. For millions of years nature exerted a gentle, unobtrusive control over its growth and evolution and innately our ancestors recognised and respected this inner dynamism. Our universe evolved as a self-organising entity, progressively developing higher and more complex forms of order and integration, and our ancestors sensed a life-principle within the earth they inhabited. A great deal of primitive worship focuses on the mysterious God of nature, whom our ancestors recognised with magnificent facility. Such worship and knowledge is sometimes naïvely dismissed as primitive idolatry; this attitude betrays not a little prejudice and a great deal of ignorance.

The God of nature served man well while man was content with his status in the 'Garden of Eden'. When man felt an urge to manipulate his destiny in the garden and proceeded to follow that instinct, things usually got seriously out of control. We lack information of the frequency of such diversions. The story of Adam and Eve in the *Book of Genesis* with its corresponding mythic tales in other cultures and religions indicate an awareness of the human tendency to outstep one's creative potential and lay claim to God's own power. The result has always been the same: destruction and disaster for the human species. The most recent of such uprisings is perhaps the best documented, a phenomenon of global impact, which is gradually unfolding its terrifying consequences.

The Contemporary Torture of Nature

Man's most recent attempt to manipulate life in the 'Garden of Eden' began in the sixteenth and seventeenth centuries:

> The notion of an organic, living and spiritual universe was replaced by that of the world as machine, and the world-machine became the dominant metaphor of the modern era. The development was brought about

by revolutionary changes in physics and astronomy, culminating in the achievements of Copernicus, Galileo and Newton. The science of the seventeenth century was based on a new method of enquiry, advocated forcefully by Francis Bacon, which involved the mathematical description of nature and the analytic method of reasoning conceived by the genius of Descartes. Acknowledging the crucial role of science in bringing about these far-reaching changes, historians have called the sixteenth and seventeenth centuries the Age of the Scientific Revolution (Fritjof Capra, *The Turning Point*, p. 38).

The new scientific attitudes and technological inventions become the modern substitutes for the mystical vision of divine truth and the sympathetic evocation of natural and spiritual forces by ritual and prayerful invocation. The new scientific mentality emerged to be grossly analytical and mathematical, compulsively rational and indiscriminately manipulative. In the words of one of its foremost proponents, the aim was to 'torture nature's secrets out of her, and render ourselves the masters and possessors of nature' (Francis Bacon). Thus, every feature of life was subject to intense scrutiny and only the scientific verification was worthy of credibility; the mysterious, the non-tangible and the unprovable were considered to be the infantile creations of ignorance and superstition; at best, religion was considered a dangerous myth. It was a highly mechanistic view of life based largely on the marriage of Newtonian physics and Cartesian philosophy.

The Newtonian-Cartesian paradigm entered its hey-day with the industrial revolution which is the parent of modern civilisation. The dark side of such growth is noticeable mainly in the exploitation of the earth's natural resources (e.g. oil, gas and water), and in the large scale pollution of our air, water and countryside. Economically, it has created an impasse where massive wealth has been tied in the hands of the few while the majority of earth's creatures live in poverty, hunger, unemployment and total degradation. Globally, it poses a serious threat to the maintenence of planetary homeostasis, dependent on very fine levels of atmospheric pressure, salt in the oceans, oxygen concentration, ammonia in the atmosphere and the existence of the ozone layer in the upper atmosphere. Perhaps, the greatest paradox of the scientific revolution is the massive amount of time, energy and resources that we human beings use in the creation of lethal weaponry which could totally exterminate life on our globe.

From a human point of view, we seem to lack an awareness of our role as agents of change in the universe. Man is now in control of forces that once controlled him or, more precisely, the creative process that formerly administered the earth and guided its affairs directly is now accomplishing this task in and through man as its conscious agent. Once a creature of earthly providence, man himself is now the expression of this earthly providence. Man has the power of life and death, not only over human life, but over the earth itself in its higher forms of life. For the first time human beings can intervene directly in the genetic process; they can destroy the ozone layer that encircles the earth; they can destroy the complex patterns of life in the seas and make our rivers uninhabitable by any form of life. The good achieved through man's technological prowess is, as yet, grimly overshadowed by its potentially disastrous consequences.

The New Ecological Consciousness

From that dark and obnoxious picture emerges a new story, a new myth to cope with the catastrophe that surrounds and impinges upon us. The story began to be written some twenty-five years ago. In 1960 alone, seventeen states in Africa declared their independence of colonial rule, a form of domination represented by 45% of the world population in 1945 but by only 3% in 1970. Between 1945 and 1965 the number of member states in the United Nations rose from 51 to 114; of the 63 new members all but 6 came from the African-Asian block; China entered in 1971.

Throughout the 1960s a new global consciousness was beginning to emerge, thanks in large measure to the scientific revolution itself, although clearly in conflict with the philosophy of that revolution. The enigma of scientific growth is nowhere more clearly depicted than in the observations of the first astronauts to land on the moon. Edgar Mitchell summarised his experience of the earth from outer space when he said: 'each man comes back with a feeling that he is no longer an American citizen – he is a planetary citizen,' and Russell Schwieckart, another astronaut wrote:

> You realise that on that small spot, that little blue and white thing, is everything that means anything to you – all history and music and poetry and art and death and birth and love, tears, joy, games, all of it on that little spot out there. . . You recognise that you are a piece of that total

life . . . And when you come back there is a difference in that world now. There is a difference in that relationship between you and that planet, between you and all those other forms of life on that planet, because you have had that kind of experience (quoted by Peter Russell, p. 4).

For many of the astronauts the journey to outer space created not merely a new perception of the earth, but generated a new awareness of the unity of the earth and the interdependence of all life-forms on the planet. What initially was a mere observation became a deeply personal and spiritual experience, which strangely and, maybe prophetically, coincides with the emergence of a new scientific consciousness, focusing attention not on the objective, quantifiable, mechanistic universe but on the subjective, emotional and pulsating world of life and movement viewed as a dynamic, living whole.

This new orientation simmered in the precognition of Teilhard de Chardin for some thirty years before the publication of his ideas after his death in 1955. In Asia, too, some creative minds were projecting new images of humanity, such as Sri Aurobindo's *The Life Divine*. In a more secular vein, Lyall Watson's *Supernature* marked a breakthrough in scientific thought and is only one of several such works published in the 1970s. James Lovelock's *Gaia: A New Look at Life on Earth* marked the first serious effort to substantiate the view that the earth is a living organism in its own right with its own life and uniqueness which cannot and should not be subjected to the dissecting, rational and analytical scrutiny of orthodox science.

According to the *Gaia hypothesis* (so called after the ancient Greek Earth Mother goddess, *Gaia* or *Ge*), the atmosphere is governed on a day-to-day basis by the many living processes on earth. The entire range of the earth's living matter, from viruses to whales, from algae to oaks, plus the air, the oceans and the land surface appear to be part of a giant system able to control the temperature and the composition of the air, sea and soil so as to maintain the optimum conditions for the survival of life on the planet. In other words, the earth acts as if it were a living, single organism and Gaia signifies the life movement (energy) which permeates the entire biosystem.

According to Lovelock, Gaia has three characteristics whose effectiveness is dependent on human co-operation and sensitivity:

1. The most important property of Gaia is the tendency to optimise

conditions for all terrestrial life. Provided that we have not seriously interfered with her optimising capacity, this tendency should be as predominant now as it was before man's arrival on the scene.

2. Gaia has vital organs at the core, as well as expendable and redundant ones mainly on the periphery. What we do to our planet may depend greatly on where we do it.

3. Gaian responses to changes for the worse must obey the rules of cybernetics, where the time constant and the loop gain are important factors. Thus the regulation of oxygen has a time constant measured in thousands of years. Such slow processes give the least warning of undesirable trends. By the time it is realised that all is not well and action is taken inertial drag will bring things to a worse state before an equally slow improvement can set in.

Our new understanding of the earth has been further enhanced by the emerging interdisciplinary study now known as *General Systems Theory*, which views the world as an interconnected hierarchy of matter and energy. According to this view nothing can be understood on its own; everything is part of a system, including individual human beings who must learn that they, too, are integral parts of this complexity and that they live or die to the extent that each individual part of the whole lives or dies. It will do little good for any individual person (or nation) to seek its own well-being by destroying the very conditions of planetary well-being. This larger vision is no longer utopian; it concerns the most basic reality there is including the water we drink, the air we breathe, the food we eat, and at a more general level, economics and politics. Any single activity must find its place within the larger pattern or it will die and, perhaps, bring down the larger life-system itself.

Humanity is part of an evolving process, where all the individual components inter-relate and interact for the growth and integration of the whole. Even opposites are viewed not in a polarising sense but as possible only in relation to each other and to the total surrounding reality. In his major work, *Living Systems*, James Miller outlines nineteen subsystems which characterise all living organisms, including the biosphere. Eight of these systems essentially portray the way all life-forms ingest, digest and excrete physical matter and energy, and a further nine are concerned with information processes, whereby knowledge of the environment is received and integrated.

Closely aligned to Miller's theory is that of Erich Jantsch in his book, *The Self-Organizing Universe*, which perceives our world evolving as a dissipative system (a term borrowed from modern biology). According to this theory the earth's energy is in a continual state of fluctuation, occasionally reaching crisis level, and always dissipating entropy (random or wasted energy). This would seem to suggest, as the Second Law of Thermodynamics asserts, that life is continually running down, moving towards more random, disorderly states. According to Jantsch, Miller and other contemporary scholars this progressive deterioration takes place only in *closed systems* and not in open ones where matter and energy are being continually exchanged with the local environment. In other words, the interaction with the environment serves to channel the entropy and thus facilitate an evolution of internal order within the organism itself. Consequently, the earth, being an open system interacts with other planetary systems in the biosphere and progressively integrates the positive and negative energies of the environment. (See more on this topic in chapter 8).

Ecology and Mysticism

One may surmise that this is a purely random coincidence. New trends in scientific research tend to suggest otherwise. A fascinating field of study showing the interaction between the new holistic science and the great mystical traditions of mankind (especially those of the east) is beginning to gather momentum. Among the leading contemporary exponents is the physicist Fritjof Capra, whose works *The Tao of Physics* and *The Turning Point* are landmarks of revolutionary proportion in our new global consciousness. Capra, apart from being a brilliant physicist, also has firsthand knowledge and experience of many of the great eastern mystical traditions. In conjunction with Walter Stace, he claims that the central core of all mystical (indeed, religious) experience is that of oneness with creation. This too, says Capra, is the goal of all scientific research, beginning with Einstein himself:

> A human being is a part of the whole, called by us 'universe', a part limited in time and space. He experiences himself, his thoughts and feelings, as something separated from the rest – a kind of optical delusion of his consciousness. This delusion is a kind of prison for us, restricting us to our personal desires and to affection for a few persons nearest to

us. Our task must be to free ourselves from this prison by widening our circle of compassion to embrace all living creatures and the whole nature in its beauty. (Words of Einstein, quoted by Russell, p. 129)

According to Capra, the rising concern with ecology, the strong interest in mysticism, the growing feminist awareness and the rediscovery of holistic approaches to health and healing are all manifestations of the same evolutionary trend. He draws on the wisdom of eastern rather than western mysticism because:

> For the eastern mystic, all things and events perceived by the senses are inter-related, connected and are but different aspects or manifestations of the same ultimate reality. Our tendency (in the west) to divide the perceived world into individual and separate things and to experience ourselves as isolated egos in this world is seen as an illusion which comes from our measuring and categorising mentality. . . Although the various schools of eastern mysticism differ in many details, they all emphasise the basic unity of the universe which is the central feature of their teaching. (*The Tao of Physics*, p. 29)

In *The Turning Point*, Capra goes on to show that the global perspective, the ability to perceive and construe reality as interrelated in a global network of interacting subsystems, is the only way forward and is increasingly being recognised as such in a variety of different disciplines, especially in science, religion, psychology, medicine and economics. Needless to say, the process is not without resistance, and the many among us with vested interests, whether individuals, corporations or nations are quick to dismiss this new vision as fantastic or even bizarre. And fittingly, Capra concludes on precisely that note:

> During the process of decline and disintegration the dominant social institutions are still imposing their outdated views but are gradually disintegrating, while new creative minorities face the new challenges with ingenuity and rising confidence.
> . . . while the tranformation is taking place, the declining culture refuses to change, clinging ever more rigidly to its outdated ideas; nor will the dominant social institutions hand over their leading roles to the new cultural forces. But they will inevitably go on to decline and disintegrate while the rising culture will continue to rise and eventually will assume its leading role. As the turning point approaches, the realisation that evolutionary changes of this magnitude cannot be prevented by short-term political activities provides our strongest hope for the future. (*The Turning Point*, p. 466)

Such is the emerging vision: earthly, global, human, ecological and yet mystical and spiritual; not, however, a spirituality away from or against the world, and not the spirituality of formal, official religion, but one at the heart of the world, passionately and compassionately committed to the evolution of life, the development of the earth and the creation of a true humanity. The global religion is an integrated religion, arising from within, based on conviction and arising from true love, with little or no institutional or legal foundation. It seeks to bring together the diversity of belief systems (expressions of the spiritual) without destroying the uniqueness of any. It seeks to build bridges between the rational and intuitive, between east and west, between poor and rich. It seeks unity of vision, not of dogma, and it tolerates whatever variety of religious expression our diversity of culture demands.

Towards an Ecological Religion

The emerging religious vision, the ecological religion, with such powerful potential to unite humankind, is a very different entity from any of the contemporary religious systems of man. But it is not a new phenomenon and, in fact, has a historical precedence which none of the formal religions can claim. It is essentially the religion of our ancestors, whose life-story unfolded in dialogue with the God of the universe, the God of nature, the God-within who forged mystical and mysterious bonds with the earth, the sky, the seasons, the animals and, finally, with one's fellow men and women. And yet, the invitation to the new global consciousness is not merely a return to the past. We are at a different point on the axis of evolution and the only authentic way is the way forward. A nuclear, global holocaust, which nobody in today's world can dismiss, would force us to start all over again, it would recreate the original search and unity, but would also condemn us to repeating the errors of our ancestors with whom we would then have lost contact.

A return to the simplicity and purity of original forms is always an attractive option, but is merely an illusive fantasy. On the other hand, the awareness that we once did share a common spiritual vision, which does not mean that our ancestors were united in every ritualistic and legal detail (quite the contrary, in fact), is a powerful motivation to enter into the new dialogue arising from the creative interaction of modern science and traditional, eastern mysticism.

Once we can shed the ideological allegiance to our own individual position, which is not heresy but rather a departure from our partial perception of the truth, then we experience the freedom and warmth of the whole truth which is global and universal, encompassing the combined religious experience of mankind. One is not suggesting a change in one's religious allegiance; the truth of any one position can lead to the whole truth, as long as we do not become imprisoned in the structures and rituals designed to give expression to the mystery from which all religion arises.

The manipulation and exploitation of human and natural resources, instigated by the technology and science of the present century in particular, has created a new awareness of man's place in nature and, paradoxically, a new awareness of the sacredness of nature. The conservation of nature along with its progressive and appropriate development, is now understood to be the basis for the harmonious co-existence of all life-forms, for the ongoing evolution of life, for peace between nations, for the redressing of imbalances between the 'haves' and 'have nots' and for a more integrated ownership of religious belief.

Both modern science and the mysticism of all ages, reminds us of our place in nature, as sons and daughters of mother earth and children of the universe. The more alienated we become from nature, the more we become strangers to ourselves and exploiters of the one who nourishes us. Life today, especially in the northern hemisphere, is false and even perverse. We can spend an entire lifetime surrounded by concrete, brainwashed by television, intoxicated with drugs, ranging from pep-pills to alcohol to heroin, dissipated by the allurements of pleasure, power and prestige. We have become a people without roots, parched for that pure spring, which nature alone can give us.

Even the gods we are brought up to worship are lifeless and morose; they are distant and unreal, institutional carcasses, speaking a language which is becoming increasingly meaningless. From the depth of this loneliness and alienation we are beginning to cry for help. The big question remaining is: will we listen to those who are offering us hope? – because they are not the gods we have so long believed in and they are not the prophets of official churches. Many of them belong to no church at all. But from the silence of their atheism arises the true God we so long ago disowned and since his Spirit blows where it wills, he now speaks a new and powerful language often in the guise of a physicist, a biologist, an eastern mystic, an ecologist, perhaps an acupuncturist or an alienated youth.

God is not dead; far from it, but as always we find Him (Her?) where we least expect, at the margins of life, among the poor, in the unexpected, in the little child or in the one who searches. Even those of us who have tried to dispense with him and make him redundant, he still haunts us.

One is not suggesting that ecology is a new name for religion. Religion without an ecological base is not true religion, because it fails to ground people in the origins of life; it fails to connect them to their environment where the creative God acts out the drama of salvation through the human interaction of man, the universe and the elemental spirits. All life is sacred and that sacredness is expressed in the interconnection and interdependence of all life-forms. The God within man is also the God within the universe. When the human spirit is in tune with the global (universal) spirit then true religion can flourish. Without this global dimension religion runs the risk of becoming a stifling ideology sheltering people from their true identity. The consequence can be a God who is less than global, a false God, and hence the idolatry which is causing such an acute crisis for religious man today.

The nature of this idolatry, which is by no means unique to our time, has been closely scrutinised by sociologists throughout the present century. We explore their contribution in the next chapter.

Bibliography

Aurobindo, Sri, *The Life Divine*, Pondicherry: Centenary Library, (no date given).

Capra, Fritjof, *The Tao of Physics*, Flamingo/Fontana, 1976.

——, *The Turning Point*, Flamingo/Fontana, 1982.

Eliade, Mircea, *Gods, Goddesses and Myths of Creation*, Harper & Row, 1967.

Fox, Matthew, *Original Blessing: A Primer in Creation Spirituality*, Bear and Co., Inc., 1983.

Griffiths, Bede, *Return to the Centre*, Collins, 1976.

Jantsch, Erich, *The Self-Organizing Universe*, Pergamon Press, 1980.

Lovelock, James, *Gaia: A New Look at Life on Earth*, Oxford University Press, 1979.

Miller, James, *Living Systems*, McGraw-Hill, 1978.

Russell, Peter, *The Awakening Earth*, Routledge and Kegan Paul, 1982.

Stace, Walter, *The Teachings of the Mystics*, New American Library, 1960.

Watson, Lyall, *Supernature*, Hodder & Stoughton, 1973.

6

The Dilemma of Religious Institutions
(Sociology)

In all living systems, whether they are embryos, landscapes or cultures, organisation limits the possibility of re-organisation.
— RENÉ DUBOS

Whereas growing civilisations display endless variety and versatility those in the process of disintegration show uniformity and lack of inventiveness. — FRITJOF CAPRA

In the great crisis of transition from the declining old to the new emerging super-system the polarisation of human souls, groups and values regularly occurs. Most persons and groups who under normal conditions are neither too saintly nor too sinful. . . tend, in the conditions of catastrophe and crisis, to polarise.
— PITRIM A. SOROKIN

IN THE SOCIAL-SCIENTIFIC STUDY of religion, the demarcation line between the anthropologist, sociologist and psychologist remains somewhat blurred, mainly because of the complex nature of the subject itself. Yet, each science extrapolates some unique features in man's religious quest and hopefully enriches our understanding of those elements which in greater or lesser measure come under scrutiny in all three sciences.

Sociology may be briefly defined as the study of the relationships existing between people living together in socially identified structures which may range from the massive anonymous group comprising a nation to the small intimate group of the family or social club.

The values which legitimise these groups along with the norms which regulate the interaction among individuals within the groups and the more elusive 'consciousness' (what Berger and Luckmann call 'knowledge') governing attitudes and expectations all fall within the ambit of sociological study.

Sociology of Religion: Historical Background

Historically, religion has been influential in the growth of social consciousness and even in today's secularised world it is dominant in determining both the quality and content of many social functions, e.g. burials, ceremonies, sects, official church organisations and the broader implications spiritually, socially and politically of being affiliated to one or other official creed. It is not surprising, therefore, that sociologists beginning with their founding fathers, Comte and Spencer, have given much attention to the religious factor in social organisation. Although sociologists of every school have studied the subject (however briefly) there is a great divergence of opinion about its place and significance in the social system.

1. *Comte and Spencer*: In their theories for a new society, both Comte and Spencer present a positive but critical analysis of religion. Both consider religion to have been the mainstay of an earlier culture now displaced by an emerging secular civilisation in which religion would become largely if not totally redundant. Although both followed similar lines there are notable differences in their approaches. Comte envisaged a positivist society, governed by scientists and intellectuals working in close liaison with industrialists. Thus, positivism would provide for society what Christianity had done for Europe right through the middle ages, creating intellectual certainty, moral consensus and social stability.

Spencer outlines a progressively developing understanding of religion, arising initially out of fear of spirits and dreams, progressing to ancestor worship, polytheism and eventually monotheism. On a first reading, Spencer seems to be very opposed to religion, gravitating towards the opinion that religion is merely a temporary support-structure until man and society reach the capacity for self-responsibility. But Spencer never goes quite that far and speaks favourably of religion as a means of fostering friendship and co-operation among human beings while also guaranteeing the retention of the most worthwhile values of the past. He also suggests, and is quite critical of the Church's negative attitude to Copernicus and Darwin, that religion could be useful in developing interest in the various enigmas that are found in the universe, a means of motivating people to initiate and support scientific enquiry.

2. *Max Weber*: The relationship between religion and social organisation was of particular interest to Weber. His basic work on this subject, *The Protestant Ethic and the Spirit of Capitalism*, is a study of the norms regulating the conduct of business in seventeenth century Europe. Weber claims that the Protestant reformers (especially Calvin) created a new work ethic, wherein business was considered a vocation *(Beruf)* and its fruits were not to be enjoyed but held in temporary stewardship. Weber then went on to formulate the hypothesis that there exists a meaningful congruence between the religious ethos of a culture and its prevailing norms of conduct. He sought to verify this proposition by a systematic analysis of other major world religions: Confucianism, Taoism, Hinduism, Buddhism and Judaism. Subsequently, in tracing the evolution of religious ideas, Weber maintains that religion tends to be a dynamic factor facilitating social change.

3. *Emile Durkheim:* None of the early sociologists contributed so much to the sociology of religion as Durkheim, whose final major work, *The Elementary Forms of Religious Life* was published in 1912. Although Durkheim himself was an agnostic, he held that religion was man's most fundamental experience, primarily a system of ideas with which individuals represent to themselves the society of which they are members.In society, sanctified by religion, Durkheim saw the origin of all man's major institutions and ideas. For Durkheim, the reality expressed by religion was a social one and society without religion seems to have been inconceivable for him.

Durkheim rejected both the animistic basis for primitive religion adopted by Spencer and E. B. Tylor and the naturalistic account expounded initially by Max Muller. He considered totemism to be the most fundamental feature of primitive religion, believing that the totem symbolises not merely the totemic principle (i.e. God) but also the clan itself, and from this observation he maintains that all religious systems have an innate potential for social organisation.

4. *Joachim Wach*: To this day, Wach is considered to be one of the

most profound and perceptive of the sociologists of religion. He tends to be critical of his predecessors especially Comte, Marx and Spencer, claiming that they held too rigidly to the enquiry into social origin, sociological structure and social efficacy of a religious group or movement. Wach has confronted the rationalistic prejudice which claims that it is the intellectual expression of religious experience alone which counts:

> The rediscovery of the central place of worship in all religion. . . was facilitated by sociological studies; it was the merit of sociological inquiries to have opened up the wide fields of social grouping of covenanting and associating, in which religious motivation plays so highly significant a part (*The Comparative Study of Religions*, p. xxxiii).

Today, two leading names in the sociology of religion are those of Peter L. Berger and Thomas Luckmann, who argue that the positivist element in the social sciences has led to a neglect of the subjectivist realm of social reality (scientifically called 'intentionality'), without which religion as a belief system cannot be fully understood. In order to construct a picture of reality for themselves, people need a belief system and, according to Berger and Luckmann, religion has a decisive role in maintaining as well as in constructing that reality. Once constructed, that strong edifice will provide an insulation from the recurring ambivalence and ambiguity of life.

However, since people at different moments of cultural evolution perceive reality differently, old constucts tend to become irrelevant and, in time, useless. The decline in religious belief and practice is new territory for contemporary sociology, Berger being one of its leading researchers. This decline, sociology would largely attribute to excessive institutionalisation of old constructs, and changing cultural (evolutionary) conditions, necessitating new models, factors which are discussed at length throughout this book.

From this historical overview we move to a general analysis of religion in its primitive and contemporary manifestations.

The Function of Religion

Since religion has existed for so long and in every human society of which we have any record, it must have an important function in people's lives and in the life of the universe. This for the sociologist is the starting point. In established societies, the function of religion can be more easily discerned and sociologists of every school have noted one or all of the following factors:

1. Religion is one of the important institutional structures making up the total social system. Unlike other institutions, such as government, economic structures and the family, it is comparatively vague, intangible and illusive. The reason for its existence seems in some strange way to be outside and beyond itself.

2. Despite this illusive nature, religion has had profound implications for human life and the growth of culture, and religious institutions have been among the most stable forms of human association, maintaining equilibrium in the social system as a whole.

3. Religion has also been characterised as embodying the most sublime of human aspirations: as being a source of public order and inner individual peace, a bulwark of compassionate and caring service, an architect of morality, a focus which evoked heroism and nobility. It has also been accused as being a stubborn obstacle to progress, often promoting fanaticism, intolerance, bigotry and open conflict between people.

4. Historically, it has served to create bonds of unity and reconciliation between peoples and nations and yet has an outstanding record for being potentially divisive, being a dominant factor in creating turmoil and warfare, examples of recent times being Northern Ireland, Iran and El Salvador.

5. *Man's need for transcendence* seems to be the basic function of his religious beliefs and practices. Wendel T. Bush (cf, Thomas F. O'Dea, p. 3) expresses it cryptically: '. . . religion is a very important part of the world of imagination that functions socially. . .' Man, in the precariousness of human existence has created an inventory to cope with what O'Dea (pp. 5-6) calls the 'breaking points' of life and its meaning:

(a) *Contingency:* Life is full of unpredictability. No matter how well planned, even with the expertise of modern technology, human hopes and aspirations are liable to be dashed or at best only partially achieved. There is a basic uncertainty in human life which St Augustine expressed poignantly when he wrote: '. . . our hearts are restless until we rest with you.'

(b) *Powerlessness:* In primitive times, man was very conscious of his total dependence on nature. Today, human beings are at the mercy of world powers and multi-national companies. And all through history, even with the abundance and progress of medical knowledge, man feels the threat of pain, suffering and death.

(c) *Scarcity*: The differential distribution of goods and values in society create an inherent feeling of frustration and deprivation. At all levels of life (even in very wealthy societies) there is a consciousness of the haves and have nots. Moreover, order implies authority, requiring control and supervision on the part of some (usually the minority) and subordination on the part of others (usually the majority). The 'just society' is an aspiration of every age and culture.

According to the sociologist, these three characteristics, contingency, powerlessness and scarcity, are permanent features in the fabric of human social interaction. They are existential characteristics of the human condition, discernible to some degree in all societies. They evoke in man a response, i.e. an effort to cope with these elements alien to the equilibrium that human beings continually seek to create so that they can control their environment. Central to this response was (and is) what Talcott Parsons calls a 'transcendental reference', a relationship with something or someone above and beyond our world capable of complementing and completing the incomplete 'sphere of meaning' that human beings perceive and feel in their individual lives and social interaction.

Religion, therefore, serves six major functions in society:

1. Important emotional aid in the face of threatening elements to the human condition. Religion provides emotional support in the face of uncertainty, consolation in the face of disappointment and reconciliation with society when alienated from its goals and expectations.

2. Through its shared beliefs and values, its cult and worship ceremonies, religion provides established points of reference creating security and identity amid the conflicts and ambiguities of life.

3. Religion sacralises the norms and values of established society, contributing to social control, aiding order and stability and facilitating the reconciliation of the deviant and alienated.

4. Religion exerts a prophetic influence, challenging individuals and institutions to a critical evaluation of standards and lifestyle. The prophetic function if properly utilised, may be an important source of social protest. The role of Christian churches in Latin America today is strongly prophetic in both word and action.

5. Religion has an important identity function, described by Davis in these words:

> Religion gives the individual a sense of identity with the distant past and limitless future. It expands his ego by making his spirit significant for the universe and the universe significant for him. (p. 531)

The identity is created initially by formal acceptance into one or other religious system and enhanced thereafter by participation in ritual and worship and accommodation of shared beliefs and values. Paradoxically, the identity may also be important through reaction to, or rejection of, one's inherited belief systems. This topic is treated elsewhere in the book.

6. Religion enhances the maturation of the individual and his passage through the various stages of growth and development. This claim is likely to evoke a variety of reactions, especially in today's western world where religion is frequently considered to be restrictive, inhibiting human growth and, perhaps, stifling it completely. There is abundant anthropological evidence to the effect that religion has greatly enhanced man's progress. Rites of Passage in many contemporary tribal religions (especially in Africa) sacralise and foster human independence, autonomy, dignity and acceptance. Religion remains a major influence for human growth and social cohesion in our world despite the significant decline in religious practice in recent decades. Finally, when one telescopes the accumulated influence of religion over the centuries of human history one can claim with a good degree of accuracy that a revived and renewed understanding of religion (rather than the death of religion) will be an important ingredient in the new society which increasing numbers of people are aspiring towards:

> The tendency towards secularisation probably cannot continue to the point where religion entirely disappears. Secularisation will likely be terminated by religious revivals of one sort or another. (Davis, pp. 544-545)

Other functional theories such as Feuerbach's projection theory, Freud's wish-fulfillment theory or Marx's 'opium of the people' theory were reviewed in chapter 3, on the psychology of religious belief. In the present chapter we are concerned with experiential, observable data, as evidenced in the religious history and practice of mankind.

The Progression of Religious Development

All religion begins in story, tales of past events, loaded with emotional import and imaginative legend and touching a core of meaning transcending time and place. Through the medium of story humankind elucidates the myth, the basic layer of spiritual consciousness, predating cult, ritual and formal religion; we have explored this material in chapter 2.

Thus, the first stage in the emergence of religion is that of story and myth. In fact the vitality of religion, its ongoing freshness, relevance and power to invigorate depends on its ability to maintain a sense of spontaneity and joy of story-telling. But human beings rarely stay long at this level. Very quickly the stories become belief systems. Comte spoke of the 'Law of Three Stages', involving a religious stage, a metaphysical stage and a positive stage. By metaphysical he envisages the development of concepts and categories leading to doctrinal definitions. The positive he identifies as a scientific mode of thought necessitating a rational (perhaps materialistic) interpretation. It is an informative model for an understanding of the development of religious ideas and systems.

Parallel to the development of belief systems are spontaneous and highly symbolic forms of ritual and ceremony. Initially these seem to have been associated with the burial of the dead and progressively came to be associated with man's natural fortunes and with significant moments in human life (Rites of Passage).

Just as myth tends to become formalised in belief patterns and norms of behaviour so ritual tends to become stylised and structured into official rites and ceremonies. And the final stage in the crystalising process is the institutionalisation of both belief and ritual in official organisations which we call *Churches*. Not alone does the process go on at the initial stages of each major world religion but continues throughout the development of that creed; indeed, it must continue if the creed is to survive; otherwise it stagnates and dies.

Applying this model to the growth and development of the Christian religion, O'Dea notes:

> Religious institutions evolve as patterns of worship – that is, as cult; they evolve at the same time as patterns of ideas, and definitions – that is beliefs; and they emerge as forms of association or organisation. Religious institutionalisation occurs on the intellectual level, the cultic level and the organisational level. These are three sides or aspects of one

developmental process. Here in the Christian case we see these three aspects as part of a whole. In the preaching we have the statement of what is believed, its first assertion in discourse. In the cultic activity we see the expression of basic attitudes in the relationship to sacred things – the re-enactment of the relationship to Jesus as Lord. In the brotherhood of believers we have the first form of organisation. From the preaching develops creeds and theology; from the brotherhood, the ecclesiastical organisation (pp. 38-39).

In order to survive, religion needs structure and organisation, but in many cases today these same survival requirements have become instruments which stultify rather than facilitate growth. Excessive institutionalisation of religion stifles the 'spirit'. The spontaneity, enthusiasm and creativity that led to the structuring in the first place is subsumed in the structure. In standardised religious practice today, e.g. the sacramental rites of the Catholic Church, the symbolic acts have lost a great deal of symbolic import; for many adherents they are merely mechanical gestures. Worse still, the routine and repetition of standardised ritual in many public services fails to touch the lives of people and even totally alienates some, especially young people.

The Tension between Spontaneity and Structure

The survival of religion seems to depend on its ability to maintain in creative tension the spontaneity, creativity and originality of new forms (and their appropriate expression) and the human urge to structure these expressions in a stable, universal format. What appeals to human beings, these things they like to embody in structures which will endure the temporariness of daily existence. It is a natural human aspiration and has the merit of allowing creativity and originality to come to full flowering and maturation. But it also embodies a fundamental flaw, which permeats every man-made institution, that structures are made to serve people's needs and not people to serve the existence of structures. Structures can so easily take over and stifle the original, life-giving spirit that led to their creation in the first place. Religion seems to be particularly prone to this dilemma which we now propose to examine in some of its expressions.

1. *The Dilemma of Mixed Motivation:*

Every religion commences with one or more charismatic figures who attract followers and give the new movement recognition and status. The original fervour and commitment which tends to be single-minded and unambiguous may last for a number of decades or even for a few centuries, as martyrdom did in early Christianity. A gradual institutionalisation of beliefs, norms and expectations initially enhances the motivation of adherents, mobilising support and interest. However, as time progresses, commitment wanes, apathy and fragmentation set in and motivation becomes difficult to sustain.

This progressive deterioration is well outlined by David Rumkorff and associates and outlined by Lawrence Cada and others. It begins with the stalemate which subtly undermines the apparent well-being of a movement during what is known as the stabilisation phase, that long period of time, perhaps a few hundred years, after the initial enthusiasm has settled down. The stalemate and apathy begin to surface in the form of doubt, restlessness and unease about the life-quality of the movement. Initially the doubt centres on surface issues and hence the name, *operational doubt*. Modifying religious garb or moving the place of worship from a church to an assembly hall are examples of the results of operational doubt. No one yet questions the actual value of the garb or of the religious exercises themselves.

A deeper level of breakdown is revealed by doubts concerning the intellectual assumptions that underlie the system and this we call *ideological doubt*. The propositional statements which rationalise and legitimise the social structures and processes undergo critical examination. Clerical celibacy and papal infallibility and the birth control controversy could be classified as issues of ideological doubt for many Catholics today.

The decline becomes more pronounced when the basic myths and beliefs of the system are seriously challenged; this we call *ethical doubt*. 'Isn't one religion as good as another?', expresses something of the confusion and disintegration which adherents may feel at this stage of doubt. Doubts about the divinity of Jesus, the virgin birth or the possibility of Jesus' resurrection, issues of modern theological diatribe, represent this level of questioning.

Frequently, the complete breakdown of the system with consequent chaos and almost total disintegration, is conceivable and this we call *absolute doubt*. None of the major world religions have been sufficiently long enough in existence for this final stage to be effected. And one wonders if it would, in fact, ever take place. Throughout its history, Christianity has had many 'Dark Ages', when corruption and disintegration were widespread, yet total obliteration never took place.

Deterioration of this type can also be a moment of grace and freedom; it can challenge and inspire. At the very least it can shock people into doing something about their predicament. The process of decay and corruption can also paradoxically legitimate the very existence of religion. Its ability to survive, to arouse new and strengthened motivation, after perhaps a whole century of chaos, seems to suggest an inherent ability to perdure on the one hand, and man's inability to live long without 'genuine' religion, on the other. The revitalisation is never completely new, but usually marks a return to the spirit and life-quality that generated enthusiasm and motivation in the first place. Therefore, the dilemma of mixed motivation really becomes the cycle of mixed motivation marking the rise-decline-revitalisation of religious belief as outlined in the accompanying diagram:

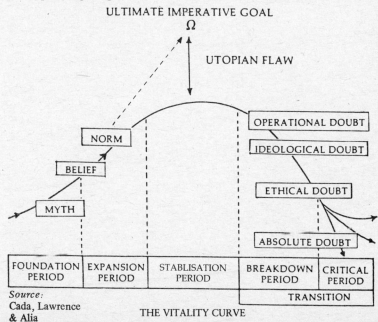

ULTIMATE IMPERATIVE GOAL

Ω

UTOPIAN FLAW

OPERATIONAL DOUBT

IDEOLOGICAL DOUBT

NORM

BELIEF

ETHICAL DOUBT

MYTH

ABSOLUTE DOUBT

FOUNDATION PERIOD	EXPANSION PERIOD	STABLISATION PERIOD	BREAKDOWN PERIOD	CRITICAL PERIOD

TRANSITION

Source:
Cada, Lawrence
& Alia

THE VITALITY CURVE

The impact of this model becomes clearer when we examine the remaining sociological dilemmas.

2. *Symbolic Dilemma: Objectivisation versus Alienation:*

Religious feelings and aspirations can only be expressed in symbolic form and this very expression also becomes the means for making possible what Eliade calls 'the prolongation of hierophanies'. Religious ritual and ceremony strives to re-enact and thus objectify the major events on which a religion is founded. The symbolism seeks to make real now what happened at some precious time in the past but also, and perhaps more important, to guarantee the survival of that once-off event, so that all generations can reap its benefits.

Implicit in these observations is a strong, social component. Religious values are shared values and the symbolic language and gesture must, therefore, have a common meaning for the participants; otherwise, it fails to convey the necessary sense of continuity and will, therefore, fail to evoke the sentiments and feelings for which it is designed. By the same token, ritual must captivate something of the originality and freshness of the founding charism and must continue to do that if it is to retain its appeal and relevance. To maintain this freshness in standardised universal structures of worship and ritual, is a difficult task.

Young people today often speak of the boredom of official church ceremonies. The language and gesture do not belong to their age or culture and hence fail to evoke in them a meaningful response. In many of our churches, ritual has become excessively stylised and fails to connect with the sublime and sacred. Sacred texts are repeated *ad nauseam*, with language and ideas which alienate people today – hatred of the world, glorification of suffering, male-domination, are frequently recurring themes. In the name of preserving tradition, the churches today run a distinct risk of destroying the best in their own tradition.

Contrary to the structured mentality of our age, religion survives and continues to grow, not in neatly-structured and universally-standardised ritual but in a mode of expression that is open and flexible to the needs and aspirations of our age and culture, and yet embodies something of the tradition of past and present in a vibrancy that evokes a positive response from people of our time. To create that happy balance is a major challenge for all the religious systems of our time.

3. *The Dilemma of Administrative Order:*
It is sometimes said that the strength of Catholicism rests in its hierarchical structure and bureaucratic organisation which are presumed to guarantee stability and growth. A glance at our vitality curve (p. 103) will reveal the wisdom of this remark and yet, its frightening potential to stifle and destroy. The progression from *myth* to *belief* to *norm* creates (spontaneously, in fact) structures which guarantee expansion and growth. One must note, however, that such structures arise out of the enthusiasm of new beginnings and must not be identified with the evangelisation of those who have not yet heard. Moreover, religious institutions are unique in so far as they cannot be studied with the same precise tools of investigation applicable to economic or government structures:

> But institutional religion itself rests upon an unstable base, since it is vulnerable to that form of breakthrough known in religious language as doubt. . . Religion once established does not provide secure and permanent answers. Life and thought continue to drive man beyond the established, institutionalised answers and their representation in religious forms. *Doubt* comes into existence as a fundamental breaking point within the religious context itself (O'Dea, p. 27).

Every religious tradition, having come through the euphoria of new beginnings moves towards the perception of itself as the source of salvation for all people. At this point it runs the distinctive risk of becoming an ideology (see p. 103) demanding a blind and irrational allegiance, which effectively stultifies the spiritual growth of its members. In the Christian tradition, Israel came to be understood as the people to which God revealed himself in an unique and special way and so the Israelite nation considered itself to be the 'chosen people'. At various moments in Christian history, e.g. the nineteenth and twentieth centuries, the concept 'chosen people' came to be understood in an exclusively sectarian way, whereby the Christian church understood itself to be the recipient of the one and only true revelation and hence the slogan: 'outside the church there is no salvation'. Modern Catholic theology, in striving to move away from this bigoted interpretation, alerts us to the original biblical meaning of the 'chosen people' to be understood *inclusively* rather than *exclusively,* as recipients of the Good News for *all* peoples rather than for their own spiritual promotion.
Two factors come into play here; firstly, the myth-belief-norm

progression needs a structure and a system if it is to flower and flourish and yet that very same structure is likely to become a major obstacle in the attainment of its full potential. Structures and systems tend to be self-perpetuating; they are notoriously slow to admit or recognise their finitude. In the majority of cases it is not the structures that fade into oblivion but rather the ideas that created the structures in the first place and which were intended to outlive those same institutions. To the best of my knowledge, social science has not yet come to grips with this dilemma.

Secondly, there is a time/cultural factor: structures which emerge in one set of conditions and in response to one set of needs often turn out later to be unwieldly instruments for handling new challenges under new conditions. This has a particular relevance to Christianity, which in the course of its early development, inherited many features of Hebraic and Greek origin and adopted a form of organisation prevalent in Roman society at that time. In terms of leadership, one notes a distinctive difference between the hierarchical model in operation in many Christian churches today and the charismatic one which seems to have dominated the early Pauline churches. This latter model may have much more in common with the new style of 'leadership-from-within' which seems to be emerging in many secular institutions today.

4. *The Dilemma of Delimitation: Concrete Definition versus Substitution of the Letter for the Spirit:*
Inspirational messages of a charismatic nature profoundly influence people and they wish to preserve this good news for posterity. From this a process of definition and concretisation emerges, not reinforced by any official authority (which usually does not exist at that early stage) but arising from the wishes of the early disciples themselves. In this way the import of the message is protected against interpretations which would transform it in ways conflicting with its inner ethos. Therefore, we notice in the history of the Christian church a continual process in which doctrine is defined in response to interpretations felt to be heretical. In fact, many better known Catholic doctrines arose from such anti-heretical polemic, especially in the Council of Trent, concerned as it was with counteracting the Protestant Reformation.

The Catholic development of doctrine offers a classic example of the dilemma of delimitation. The Second Vatican Council is one of the first occasions in which the Catholic Church departed significantly from anti-heretical polemic and sought to proclaim the message of its founder in a manner relevant to the present age. The fact that earlier Councils, for the greater part, were concerned with the defensive safeguarding of orthodoxy, has given the Catholic Church a particularly strong legalistic and oppressive image. The letter of the law (which has not always been the *letter*, never mind the *spirit* of Scripture), and the impact of canon and dogma is strong in Catholic tradition. Hence we find that a great deal of missionary work, especially in Africa, was not an evangelisation which sought to integrate local values, but rather one which simply imposed western Christian values, symbols and ritual, some of which were totally at variance with the mind and ethos of African culture. Precisely because of such rigid and unreflective fidelity to the letter of the law, the spirit of Christianity, its tolerance, love and compassion has often taken second place and sometimes has been totally overshadowed by external frivolities.

Since the Second Vatican Council the Catholic Church has been much more open to experimentation and flexibility, especially in its liturgy and pastoral action. However, the tight reins of morality and law still raise their ugly heads and calls to 'tighten-up' are disturbingly frequent among clergy and people alike. A creative tension between spirit and law (cf. St Paul in the letters to *Galatians* and *Romans*), is inherent to mature religious development. To maintain that tension rather than seek its resolution seems to be one of the great challenges for religious protagonists of every age and culture.

5. *The Dilemma of Power: Conversion versus Coercion:*
Commitment to one or other religious system is based first and foremost on an 'act of faith'. It is commitment to God (or gods) and to the transcendent values which makes the relationship with that deity an integral and 'meaning-producing' dimension of life. Inherent, too, to this commitment is a social aspect; conversion involves to a greater or lesser degree a new relationship with one's fellow men and women, even if this implies segregation from society for a life of silence and seclusion (hermits). The initial fervour is neither legalistic nor moralistic and is not particularly concerned with structure or organisation.

Progressively, personal faith is supplemented by public opinion and current ideas of respectability and the approval and support of accepted authority take on a gradual and increasing importance. In this way, religion begins to relate to other institutions of society and to cultural values. In time, it will accommodate the standards of society, and religion and power may coalesce, as has happened frequently in the western world. The anti-world stance which we wrongly attribute to early Christianity is, in fact, much more the product of post-Reformation times, when the Catholic Church in particular, perceived itself as the depository of pure Christianity and sought to innoculate and shelter all its members against the heretical influences of the secular world.

When religion becomes aligned to earthly power or even when it borrows its models from secular institutions it loses much of its real vitality – *to conscientise man towards an awareness of, and a response to, his role in the plan of creation*. In responding to this task it performs a transforming effect on at least four different levels of human life:

1. It provides *a dramatic design*, symbolically transforming human experience, helping to create amid the chaos and confusion of life a sense of purpose, process and passage aimed at greater harmony and integration for human beings and their world.

2. Religion is also *a defensive system*, providing an array of beliefs and attitudes which help to defend us againt vexing doubts, anxieties and aggressions. Many religious systems have specific structures (e.g. Confession in the Catholic Church) to facilitate the release of painful and potentially destructive emotional blocks.

3. Religion also serves as *a directive system*. Every religion embodies a moral code, aimed at human and earthly well-being, striving to safeguard dignity and integrity and aimed at an improved quality of life for everybody inhabiting our universe.

4. Religion involves *a symbol economy* creating a climate for reflective dialogue with those elements of life which fascinate and frighten; which touch our inner core, yet transcend our deepest hopes and aspirations.

In serving these four purposes and, perhaps, others, religion functions primarily and most appropriately in a relationship with people at the 'ordinary' level of their daily experience. The ministers of religion, whether pope, bishops or clergy, have no impact as members of a power structure. They may be perceived as powerful by virtue of office – and frequently have been – but their real influence is borne out in their own godliness and in their ability to respond to man's godliness through the vehicle of the common humanity of both giver and receiver. The dynamism of religion rests in the human/spiritual interaction, in the common struggle of searching amid ambiguity and ambivalence and in the common joy of discovering together the truth which sets us free.

The development of democratic society in the west owes much to religion, and the prophetic stance taken by religious protagonists today in parts of Latin America and Africa is likely to have profound implications for future generations living in those continents. The evidence to hand of how religion influences and is influenced by society and the institutions of society is far from complete. Nonetheless it does furnish insights and information which greatly enrich our understanding of religion.

Positively and negatively, religion has had profound influence. Positively it has enhanced man's control of his life and environment, furnished social and cultural values which have bound people together in brotherhood and harmony, created an environment of care, respect and concern, and has served as a cathartic outlet for fear, alienation, aggression and grief.

Negatively, it has frequently created friction, tension and open conflict. At a more personal level, it has served as an escape from reality and led to the harbouring of neurotic fear, excessive guilt and repressed anger. It has created power structures and legalistic, moralistic mores which have sought to absolutise human powers in the name of supernatural rights. It has often led to racialism, bigotry and fanaticism.

Faced with the sociological evidence one is left with two distinct impressions:

(a) On a general universal level, religion has contributed significantly to the development of human progress and to the growth of civilisation.

(b) In terms of its particular manifestations, there are abundant examples of its negative power to alienate and oppress, to dominate and delude people into infantile thought and action. One wonders if this latter is, in fact, a negative power or an abuse of the positive power which is religion's real essence. In raising that question one is going beyond the sociologist's brief whose task is to analyse nonjudgementally the facts he observes.

In concluding, we acknowledge the wealth of insight and understanding which the sociologist brings to our field of study, especially the critique of established religion, its negative power to stifle and enslave and its greater creative power to invigorate and enliven.

Bibliography

Berger, Peter, *A Rumour of Angels*, London: Allen Lane, 1970.
——, *The Sacred Canopy*, Penguin, 1973.
Cada, Lawrence & Alia, *Shaping the Coming Age of Religious Life*, Seabury Press, 1979.
Davis, Kingsley, *Human Society*, Macmillan Co., 1948.
Eliade, Mircea, *Patterns in Comparative Religion*, Sheed & Ward, 1958.
Luckmann, Thomas, *The Invisible Religion*, Macmillan, 1967.
O'Dea, Thomas F., *The Sociology of Religion*, Prentice-Hall, 1966.
Wach, Joachim, *The Sociology of Religion*, University of Chicago Press, 1944.
——, *The Comparative Study of Religions*, Columbia University Press, 1958.
Wilson, Bryan, *Religion in Sociological Perspective,* Oxford University Press, 1982.

7

Grappling with Creative Mystery
(Theology)

Must then a Christ suffer in torment in every age to save those who have no imagination! — GEORGE BERNARD SHAW

When dogma is severed from its root in religious imagination it becomes merely a counter in an intricate intellectual chess-game or a piece of outright ideology. — RAY L. HART

That which I have to prove by argument has no immediate reality for me. — PAUL TILLICH

No revelation is received as an answer until a question has been experienced. — JOHN SHEA

THEOLOGY is essentially a Christian concept, derived from the Greek combination of *theos* meaning 'God' and *logos* meaning 'word'. In the early centuries of the Christian church theology was closely linked with the spiritual life, characterised by different stages of 'perfection,' the highest being the monastic state. Spirituality consisted primarily of meditation on the Scriptures, seeking true wisdom for the salvation of one's soul.

Early Christian theology employed Greek language and ideas to express its basic truths and doctrines. On the basis of Aristotelian categories theology was classified as a subaltern science. For St Thomas Aquinas theology is an intellectual discipline, born of the meeting of faith and reason: faith seeking understanding *(fides quaerens intellectum)*, a definition that has prevailed to modern times. Since the Council of Trent theology has increasingly become an ancillary discipline of the magisterium of the Catholic Church to

(a) define, present and explain revealed truths, (b) examine doctrine, defending those that are true and denouncing those considered to be false and (c) teach revealed truths authoritatively.

The developments of the twelfth century sought to give theology a scientific status according to the rational understanding of the time. Spirituality then became divorced from theology, and over the centuries tended to be identified with the private, personal, devotional aspects of the faith. Discourse about Cɔd based on what we can know of him through nature was called *natural theology,* considered to be more philosophical then genuinely theological.

In the Christian context, theology presupposes faith. In the light of this faith, which it claims to be a gift, freely given, it seeks to understand what God has revealed to us initially through the Scriptures and subsequently through the church's teaching based on her interpretation of God's divine word. Theology, therefore, starts with *revelation,* what our faith informs us of what God has manifested of himself and his will for us through the sacred Scriptures.

This brief excursus provides the backdrop for an exploration of theology today and its relation to religion.

The God-Question in World Religion

Theology, therefore, refers to the development of religious doctrine, seeking to explain and expound the relationship and consequent interaction between believers and the divinity in which they profess belief. Theological reflection begins with revealed data as outlined in the sacred writings of each major religion: the Christian Bible, the Hindu Vedas, Brahams and Upishands, the Buddhist Pali Canon of Hinayanan Buddhism and the Sutras of the Mahayana school, the Taoist *Tao Te Ching,* the Confucian *Lun Yu* or confucian analects, the Muslim *Quran* and so forth. All religions consider their scripture to transcend time and culture and they use them as a permanent source of wisdom and inspiration.

Theological discourse in every religion starts with the nature of the divine and its relationship to our world. Contending with the mysterious nature of God, all religious systems use concepts and ideas which boggle the mind and bewilder the imagination. Christianity posits one God, consisting of three persons who communicate with our universe in the capacity of creative Father, Redemptive Son and unifying Spirit. Hinduism also believes in one God who manifests his presence in several categories of deities; the three most worshipped divinities in India today are Shiva, Vishnu and the Divine Mother. Since each syllable of the ancient sanskrit language is considered to be the name of a god, every word and object is considered to have a corresponding deity.

According to Buddhism, the Budda is the enlightened one, and for all Buddhists, the path to enlightenment. Buddhist writings are peopled with all kinds of gods, spirits and demons, but the Budda is considered to be above all gods. Buddhism seeks to transcend the worship of gods; it does not deny their existence but claims that they have no spiritual power. In Islam, Allah, too, is considered to be superior to the many other 'gods' posited by that system. Taoism has a distinctly non-personal concept of God, the *Tao*, a divine principle which informs and underlies nature and out of it issues the myriad things that make up the natural world (something akin to the *Logos* of John's Gospel). Enlightenment according to Taoism, is the attainment of harmony with the Tao.

The God-question has an inexhaustible fascination for the theologian. Man's search for ultimate meaning and his hunger for ultimate knowledge create the ongoing theological search. We want to know more about God and it seems there will always be more to know, especially when we start relating the diverse wisdom of all the world religions, a theological discourse which has scarcely begun. And yet, the theologian is not the cherished exponent of religious truth in any religious system; neither is the official church (except, perhaps, in the case of Christianity). An awareness of the divine, a personal relationship with God, is considered to be the way to enlightment, acquired by the practitioner who enters into the religious process via prayer, meditation, contemplation or by whatever name the spiritual communication is designated in the various religions. In other words, personal experience, rather than intellectual knowledge or consent, is considered to be the appropriate means of knowing God.

Here, we note an important parallel with our primitive ancestors whose awareness of God was largely if not exclusively natural, gleaned from daily perception of, and interaction with, their natural environment, and absorbed via myth and ritual. Speculations about God's existence, his nature or even his relationship with the world, was not pursued. Nor should we be too fast to suggest that our primitive ancestors were intellectually incapable of such reflection and speculation; their perception of life was totally different from ours. The management of life rather then speculation about its existence was their main pre-occupation. Could it be that the intellectual search for ultimate meaning is an abberation in an exclusively intellectualised culture. Perhaps, our philosophical speculation, which since the sixteenth century seems bent on disproving God rather than proving his existence, is not the appropriate vehicle to discover the true God and his plan for the universe?

The Presence of God in Created Reality

All the eastern religions are at variance with Christianity in their understanding of the divine-human encounter. Christianity is unique in its human embodiment (incarnation) of God in the world, although, historically, it has not always been faithful to the radical demands of that event. The divine rather than the incarnate Christ tends to hold the exalted position, although the theology of the past twenty years has sought to rectify this. Islam and Judaism reject the idea of incarnation and both Hinduism and Buddism postulate many incarnations, with little apparent power to influence human or earthly affairs. In general, eastern religion focuses on the human inability to codify or classify the divinity; any attempt to do so, they consider to be idolatry. Yet, it is apparent that the God or gods of eastern religions are in touch with human affairs, but their influence is quite vague and ill-defined.

From this brief outline, we detect a world-wide fascination with the idea of an ultimate power, perhaps personal, but not necessarily so, which, in one form or another, has formally entered our world and continues to influence the plan of creation and human destiny. All religions are one in their belief in an ultimate God, but vary considerably in what they consider this being to be and how he impinges on human and earthly life.

In the east, the goal of *satiori* (meditation) is the liberation of the human being from the limitations of time and space. Like traditional Christianity, the great eastern religions tend to exhibit an anti-world bias, a trait which is most noticeable in Islam. Contrary to the west, however, the east has a distinctly positive view of the 'unity of all life-forms,' a feature which Capra explains in these words:

> The most important characteristic of the eastern world view – one could say the essence of it – is the awareness of the unity and mutual inter-rela-

tion of all thing and events, the experience of all phenomena in the world as manifestations of a basic oneness. All things are seen as interdependent and inseparable parts of this cosmic whole; as different manifestations of the same ultimate reality. The eastern traditions constantly refer to this ultimate, indivisible reality which manifests itself in all things and of which all things are parts. It is called *Brahman* in Hinduism, *Dharmakaya* in Buddhism, *Tao* in Taoism (*The Tao of Physics,* p. 141).

Chinese Zen is particularly strong on this fundamental unity of all reality.

In the theology of the early Christian church and in the writings of the great Christian mystics one detects the same sense of the spirit of God pervading and uniting all reality. As a religious system, Christianity, however, has tended to emphasise a dualistic approach not inherent in its own biblical origins but inherited from Greek thought in which it sought to articulate its developing theology. The Christian message still smacks of such artificial dichotomies as body versus spirit, death versus life, God versus man, natural versus supernatural, church versus world. In the post-Reformation era, these opposites became very pronounced as the Catholic Church proclaimed itself to mankind as the only faith through which people could be saved. Recent trends in Christian theology – secularisation, political liberation – re-affirm strongly the sacredness of the world and of the human endeavour of this earth.

The Concept of Revelation

No theological dialogue between east and west can become possible till we address the subject of *revelation* (a word not used in non-Christian faiths), a divine inspiration and confirmation to which each religion lays exclusive claim. We briefly outline what the concept signifies for the different religions:

Shintoism: The *Kojiki* and the *Nihongi,* both completed at the beginning of the eight century AD are considered to be authoritative records (pure Shinto) of the ancient religion, but not divinely inspired. Such divine inspiration is considered to be unnecessary because Shintoism maintains that the natural man is in direct communion with the divine force of nature and, consequently, it does not feel the need for special documents authenticating a marked theophany or direct divine manifestations. In Shintoism, seers, but not texts, are considered to be inspired.

Confucianism: This system too maintains a form of indirect revelation. Its sacred documents are regarded as human productions, having revelation value in so far as they maintain that God, in a general and indirect way, raises up rulers and sages to lead and teach the people aright. Once again, people rather than texts are the medium of God's message.

Taoism: This belief maintains that the universe reveals its secrets to the one who by peaceful receptivity allows nature to speak, so that its *Tao* or *Way* is learned by mystic sympathy. Taoism is not based on any divine message but arises from an intuitive apprehension of reality. *Tao* is immanent in all things, working in and through everything and capable of acting upon people from any point or object in creation. Taoism is, therefore, a supremely natural religion.

Hinduism: According to the eighth-century Indian theologian, Shankara, *Brahman* (the ultimate supra-personal reality and inner essence of all things) alone is real, the subsistent spirit immanent in the universe. Because everything else is mere illusion (including man), Brahman is incomprehensible to the human mind, but may be known intuitively through mystical experience. Although the *Vedas* are considered to be inspired they are not regarded as embodying revelation. They are meant to be prayed or chanted and thus facilitate a communication with Brahman.

Even to this day, the concept of revelation in Hinduism has not been satisfactorily explained. Hinduism tends to be an extremely pragmatic religious system; in fact, many Hindus do not consider it religious in the western sense. If it works it is considered useful and hence serves to facilitate communication with the divine; if it does not work it is either altered or changed as the mood suits. Hinduism is not strictly a religious system, but a massive conglomerate of religious sub-systems.

Buddhism: After its founder's death, Buddhism developed into two main schools, the *Hinayana* and the *Mahayana*. The former considers itself to be the orthodox school which sticks to the letter of the Buddha's teaching whereas the Mahayana, which is the more widespread today, displays a greater flexibility, believing that the spirit of the doctrine is more important than its original formulation.

The *Hinayana* brand (better known today as Theravada Buddhism) tends to be predominantly monastic and seeks enlightenment through mystical experience. According to the Theravada tradition our individual existence is inevitably a life of suffering because it involves unsatisfied craving, but there is a way out of this suffering by a special path of mental and moral discipline, leading to a supranormal state of mystic contemplation *(samádhi)*. The culmination of this experience is a state *(nirvana)*, superior even to that of the gods, for they are also subject to the law of suffering, reaping only a temporary reward in heaven for good deeds performed in an earlier existence. Rather than a revelation from the gods, Budda felt that he had discovered a truth which people could reach through their own mental effort within the life process. Theravada meditation has as its goal the attainment of enlightenment or Buddahood, thus bringing to an end human individuality and human suffering.

The *Mahayana,* on the other hand, claims that the Budda is the absolute and supreme reality of the universe and totally beyond human knowledge. However, the Budda could reveal himself to the purest of creatures not via sacred texts but on the plane of the imagination as truth, bliss or supreme goodness. The Mahayana school is known as the Great Vehicle of Buddhism because it offers its adherents a great variety of methods or skilful means to attain enlightenment (Buddahood). These range from doctrines emphasising religious faith in the teachings of the Budda to elaborate philosophies involving concepts which come very close to modern scientific thought. Mahayana Buddhism is quite a practical, secular religious system.

Zoroastrianism, Judaism, Islam and Christianity: All these religions are based on the belief that God has spoken directly to man and consider their respective sacred texts to be the vehicles of this revelation; they consider such texts to be directly inspired. In all cases the supreme God is considered to be a *personal* revealer.

Sikhism: This is one of the most recent religions (fifteenth century), based mainly on a combination of Islam and Hinduism, owing its origin to a direct personal revelation to its founder Nanak (1469-1538). Sikhism seeks to overcome the divisions and bitternesses caused by religious differences and hence posits a God, the True Name, above and beyond all religious gods, yet, immanent in creation.

To synchronise or reconcile the different understandings of revelation would be a major task, demanding many rather than one scholarly work. Yet, no theology of religion is possible until this task is done. One is not suggesting an outcome of agreement or unanimity. The brief excerpts above clearly indicate extraordinary differences ranging from the vague, ill-defined ideas of Hinduism, to the divine revelation of Zoroastrianism, Judaism, Islam and Christianity. How does the theologian reconcile these differences; is it even appropriate to suggest a reconciliation?

Perhaps such diversity is an inherent element in the process of life and religion. Could this not be the legitimate differentiation and diffusion arising from the course of evolution itself? Anthropologically, religion seems to have arisen simultaneously in many parts of the inhabited earth. We have some indications of common threads. Most groups seem to have practised magic (in a variety of forms), worshipping the sun, moon and stars, and expressed their religious aspirations in Paleolithic art form. During all this time, however, ritual and worship was extremely varied in type and expression. Finally, whether they worshipped one God or many continues to be a debated question. While, apparently relating to a divinity they felt to be personal, we have little evidence to suggest that our ancestors considered this God to be a *person*. The suprapersonal nature of God, immanent in the world but yet transcending it, an understanding still retained in some of the great eastern religions, seems to be the image most lucidly portrayed in primitive mythology.

Revelation from Within

The unity-in-diversity as portrayed in our religious heritage may serve as our most appropriate starting point. Across time, culture and religious expression stretches man's need for transcendence; this is the point of departure. It does not seem even appropriate to suggest that there is *one* God towards which we all aspire. In a sense does not this concept arise from a human need for neat, uniform solutions, our tendency to view reality as a *Gestalt*. Why cannot we posit God as 'many' or as a 'world power' (de Chardin)? Is it because we have a compulsive need to perceive God as personal, this being our supreme, integrative projection of reality?

We all realise that the human peception of the person is not that of the totality of personhood and every religion that accepts a personal revelation acknowledges that the personhood of God, while incorporating all that is human, far exceeds anything we can think of or imagine. According to Paul Tillich, our efforts to personalise

God accounts for a good deal of atheistic protest:

> The protest of atheism against such a highest person is correct. There is
> no evidence for his existence, nor is he a matter of ultimate concern.
> God is not God without universal participation. 'Personal God' is a
> confusing symbol (pp. 245).

Perhaps, the eastern religions have much to teach us in postulating
the supreme God to be above all that we can think or say of God,
acknowledging as the eastern religions do, that this same God can
be, and is, immanent in creation and, in a special way, in people.

The more we reflect on the God-question, especially in the
rational mode of philosophy and theology, the more baffling it
seems to become. Once again, are we not being reminded to observe
how God became real for our ancestors and to reflect on the fact
that the living God survived for some 60,000 to 70,000 years without a formal religious system? In chapter 1, we said that man creates
religion in order to articulate his relationship with the God within
himself and within the world. In retaining the strong, individual
dimension, eastern religions and Christianity teach us something
important about our initial religious awareness of the God-within-
the-self. It needs to be stated immediately that all the religions, with
the notable exception of Taoism, have seriously departed from the
primitive understanding of the God-within-nature (life).

Initially, fundamentally and archetypally, belief in God comes
from within, individually and communally (i.e. man interacting with
creation). If the basic revelation is from *within* how do we reconcile
this with the formal divine revelation envisaged in all the major
religious systems?

According to Karl Rahner (p. 16), man's *natural* situation is to
be listening for a personal, historical revelation from God. 'Man,'
he says, 'is essentially and always a listener for a possible revelation
from God.' J. P. Mackey echoes a similar note and goes so far as to
suggest that we should cease from using the term 'revelation' and
replace it by 'faith' which he feels gives rise to expectations of
revelation:

> . . . faith is the more fundamental concept of the two, revelation the
> more secondary and derivative; faith gives rise to expectations of revela-
> tion and to revelation-talk in general and it is not the case that revelation
> gives rise to faith (quoted by Thompson, p. 170).

These observations lead us to postulate with William Thompson that revelation concerns the 'available God' (Gordon Kaufman) and not God in the fullness of his reality:

> As such revelation really concerns the question of God as that God impinges on human consciousness. Whatever else revelation may mean it at least affirms a human consciousness capable of receiving a divine revelation. If this were consistently thought through, it might clarify some of the questions still debated in theology about the nature of revelation (Thompson, p. 163).

Our fragmentary evidence suggests that primitive man was the recipient of God's revelation in ways which left him in no doubt about the existence of God. The means of revelation were appropriate for the faith of man at that stage of human evolution. Man lived in close contact with nature, which, in turn became the *locus* of God's action in the lives of primitive people. At a later stage in human development, when religion was formalised, revelations from God became more explicit, firstly through people specially chosen to be God's instruments (prophets or seers) and finally through an incarnation or embodiment of God himself. All three stages can be detected in the Christian Bible:

1.   The story of *Genesis* is a mythic account of the divine initiative in creating the world, and man's failure to respond appropriately. The writer(s) is not interested in historical, scientific detail, but tells a story, in poetic narration, full of feeling and conviction – an experiential expression, acknowledging a God of creative goodness but also a God of retributive justice.

2.   There is then a long prophetic tradition from Moses through Aaron, Jeremiah and so on, whereby God reveals himself as a loving but distant God, disclosing himself and his plan mainly through selected individuals.

This seems to be the stage at which many of the great eastern religions are still resting. From a Christian prespective, one wonders (and this observation has no judgemental intent) if development in these systems has not been hindered or even arrested. Is one to expect that they should have, or, perhaps, are still destined to become more personalised, more humanised? One is not suggesting that Christianity has achieved this state; theoretically, yes, but in practice, definitely not. Ghandi's assertion that he liked our Christ but not our Christians 'because they are so unlike your Christ', is a painful reminder to Christians how a religious system can, in fact, destroy the ultimate revelation it is intended to embody and portray.

3. Finally, there is the epiphany of God himself in the totality of human nature, the incarnation of God. Christian theology has faithfully proclaimed Jesus as the full revelation of Godhead, but only in the course of the present century has it done justice to Jesus as the fullness of *life for man,* endowing the human condition with the power of his risen spirit for the rest of time.

An Evolutionary Understanding of Revelation

The Christian model has been chosen mainly because it depicts in clearest relief (for the present author, at least) the intimate link between evolution on the one hand, and revelation on the other. John Macquarrie, more than any other theologian, has grappled creatively and imaginatively with this concept and his thinking merits some attention. For Macquarrie, the essence of existence is *Being,* which he describes as the *incomparable that lets-be and is present in and manifest to all creation* (p. 105). All created things, including man, evolve from the letting-be of being; while this 'letting-be' is creative and free it is also destined towards, what de Chardin would call, the Omega point.

We are not talking about *predestination.* Macquarrie's resolution of this dilemma is quite ingenious. He posits God the Father as primordial being, the ultimate letting-be, the origin and source of all that is. All life-forms, therefore, have been informed by the creative divine touch; all life is sacred and ultimately destined to its inherent spiritual fulfilment. Undoubtedly, life and our universe could conceivably have other origins, another type of evolutionary course, another divine plan devoid of suffering and ambiguity. But then, it would not be a free creation; there would be no evolution, no 'letting-be'. A predetermined universe could have many beautiful qualities, no war, death, pain or suffering, but then creation would only be a puppet in the hands of a manipulative, slavish creator. The creator of such a universe would be a God of slavery rather than a God of *freedom.*

Any diminution of the absolute freedom of creation – with the risks and all the negative possibilities that follow – is ultimately a diminution of God too. Despite all its imperfections and limitations, our present world seems to be the only possible one for a God who creates in absolute and radical freedom; it is the only possible universe in which man can be fully and freely involved, a universe whose progress is not facilitated by divine interventions (which also would be an insult to man's freedom) but by the daily human task of building up in a spirit of love, care and compassion.

Creation is a reflection of God's goodness and man's creativity. The absence of goodness and the marks of ugliness are living proof of man's radical freedom with the implicit risk of totally destroying the earth we inhabit. Even if this were to happen, with the impending threat of a nuclear holocaust, lower forms of life would again emerge in a short number of years and human beings would again inhabit the earth probably within four or five hundreds years. In other words, what previously evolved over millions of years in the divine 'letting-be' would now repeat itself in a few hundred years (which is but a mere second in the evolutionary-creative time-scale), thus catching up with evolution where it had been halted by the negative consequences of human freedom. Man's ultimate destructiveness, although lethally potential in human terms, cannot and will not halt the ultimate purpose of the divine letting-be. It is a sobering thought!

Why, then, does God intervene, as he has done in all the major religious systems of man, each recording the disclosure of the divine plan through an incarnation, embodiment or presence, whether by a deified figure or a prophetic person. Again, we take our working premise from Macquarrie's description of Jesus as *Expressive being,* as distinct from the Father whom he calls *Creative being.*

The Messiah-figures of all the great world religions appear within a time-span of 3,500 years (approximately), which is merely 0.6% of human history alone (starting from *Homo Erectus, c.* 500,000 years ago). It would seem, therefore, that the years, 2000 BC – 1500 AD, mark a maturing stage in human evolution in which God reveals himself in a mode confirming and affirming the beings of his creation, co-terminus with man entering a new mode of self-consciousness. According the Macquarrie, Expressive being is:

> God in one of his ways of being... expressing more adequately the immanence of God in creation... The primordial being of the Father, which would otherwise be entirely hidden, flows out through expressive being to find its expression in the world of beings (p. 203).

While none of the great eastern religions has a divine embodiment or incarnation as explicitly as that of Christianity, they all quite definitively assert God's immanence in creation and his ability to express and communicate his being in and through the creative process. Indeed, Taoism could be considered to be the most incarnational of all religions now in existence, and a dialogue between Taoism and Christianity has vast potential for the type of global, ecumenical breakthrough so acutely needed in today's world.

The incarnation, therefore, should not be viewed in exclusively biblical or theological terms. It is also an anthropological event affirming man in his human and spiritual development, redeeming (that is restoring and renewing) his creative energies and preparing him for a new stage in the evolutionary process.

This new stage has been subjected to many analyses and expressions in the twenty centuries of Christendom. We can see it as the basis of eschatological thought and apocalyptic concern in the New Testament and at various points in the history of Christianity. In religion and science alike we detect, over the past hundred years, new thresholds in human psychic development, achievements which many people view with great scepticism while others cautiously admit that these 'gifted' individuals are the first fruits of man's next evolutionary stage.

According to Macquarrie's interpretation of the Christian vision, we have already entered this phase through what Christianity calls the coming of the Holy Spirit, whom Macquarrie describes as *Unitive Being*. The unity which the Spirit builds up, says Macquarrie, is a higher unity than would have been possible had being never moved out of primordial being through expressive being. Relating this observation to our earlier reflection on man as the one who waits and listens for a revelation (Rahner), we deduce that those of us who live in the era of the Holy Spirit are invited to relate to and communicate with God in a new, supra-human way thus presuming a further stage in our evolutionary development also. This understanding is also borne out in chapters 14-17 of John's Gospel where Jesus emphatically speaks about the necessity of his departure so that the Spirit may come, the one who will lead mankind into the *whole* truth (Jn 16:13).

While not being clear on every detail, one can scarcely doubt the fact that the incarnation of God in Jesus Christ is co-terminus with a major shift, the creation of a new threshold, in the evolutionary growth of humankind. One would expect a similar transition in the other major world religions. This may be gleaned from the cultural vitality of Taoism and in the potentially creative effect of eastern religion on western science and culture, while noting that traditonal, 'exclusive' forms, such as, Hinayana Buddhism and the loosely-knit Hinduism, are losing their cultural influence, thus highlighting the need for a new quality of religion. Whether or not a new global religion is on the brink of emergence is purely a matter for speculation; one may surmise that this is likely and appropriate, or alternatively, that man living in the era of the Holy Spirit, does not need formal religion and can well survive without it, which human beings have in fact done for some 50,000-60,000 years of their history on this earth.

The development of grass-roots communities in the emerging churches of Africa and Latin America, with the emphasis on shared values, beliefs and worship of local, neighbourly groups, may well signal the new style religion where 'small is beautiful'. However, the global coming-together of mankind, reinforced in an unique way by the communication revolution of the past twenty years, is also likely to lead to the creation of globally shared values and beliefs, a process that will take a great deal longer than the local community based endeavours which are already well under way.

Is Christian Revelation Unique?

In recent centuries, the Catholic Church more than any other has insisted on the uniqueness of its own Christian revelation and its superiority to every other religious system. The first move away from this rather sectarian, triumphalist stand came with the *Declaration on the Relationship of the Church to Non-Christian Religions* from the Second Vatican Council, declaring that:

> The Catholic Church rejects nothing which is true and holy in these religions. She looks with sincere respect upon the ways of conduct and of life, whose rules and teachings which, though differing in many particulars from what she holds and sets forth, nevertheless often reflect a ray of that truth which enlightens all men. . .
>
> The Church, therefore, has this exhortation for her sons: prudently and lovingly, through dialogue and collaboration with the followers of other religions, and in witness of Christian faith and life, *acknowledge, preserve* and *promote* the spiritual and moral goods found among these men, as well as the values of their society and culture. (Abbott, pp. 662-663, *emphasis mine*)

The dialogue and collaboration envisaged by the Second Vatican Council has scarcely begun. Where to begin and how to begin is the big question which Walbert Buhlmann has tried to address in a recent work:

> The problem is a new one in theology. It is a consequence of the broadening of our horizons to include the other religions. As late as twenty years ago most manuals and monographs considered themselves well acquitted to make an ecclesiocentric presentation of the Judaeo-Christian revelation and be done with the matter. In this respect the science of comparative religions was far in advance of theology. Writing at the turn of the century, M. M. Mueller considered it 'the worst heresy' to hold that God had revealed himself to one people alone, to the Jews. God would have had to ignore and despise non-Jews and non-Christians, who have constituted the major portion of humanity from the very beginning. Is that really something to expect from God? (pp. 208-9)

Buhlmann considers salvation history and revelation to be coincident and co-extensive, and claims that there are salvific experiences before, during and after the Judaeo-Christian era. He rejects the usual distinctions between natural and supernatural, substantive and partial, biblical and non-biblical (illumination). However, he still feels compelled to retain a preferential Christian slant in his explanation of universal revelation:

> Naturally, God's revelation in the various religions occurred in various stages of development, and in increasing clarity, from unexpressed surmises about the ultimate meaning of life, to the express words of a 'prophet', to the religious rites of a people, to the Old Testament revelation and the unique self-communication of God in Jesus Christ and its perfection in the Parousia (p. 209).

It is not, however, in the New but in the Old Testament that Buhlmann discovers the origins of a new understanding of revelation:

> Comparisons will remain open! But in them all, one thing is undeniable: that the Old Testament can perform the function of a model for many purposes of comparison. The other religions may be bearers of revelation. . . but the Old Testament is clearly something more. Except for Islam which the Bible partly inspired, no other religion rallied to monotheism in a manner so theologically unambiguous, and so morally demanding, and heralded monotheism as the coming form of human religion, as did the Old Testament.
> A further advantage of the Old Testament is the deep-dyed mark of

its messianic expectation – beginning with the journey of Abraham. . .
fulfilled in Jesus Christ. Of course, hope of liberation from evil, and the
expectation of salvation – utopians – are essential categories of all religions. . . But along with the hope, many religions taught their adherents
an attitude of acquiescence and passivity, of addiction to miracles and
wonders, and thus estranged their own expectations. The Asiatic
religions were by and large the prisoners of cyclic thought; the African
religions looked for a return to the primordial. Neither, therefore, had
any concept of a clear eruption into a new, coming time (p. 214).

Because of its highly developed monotheism and specific future
orientation, the Old Testament revelation, which finds its perfect
expression in the New Testament, is put forward as a model for all
revelation. Because monotheism is so central to Buhlmann's perception of religion, the divine self-enclosure of the Old and New
Testaments cannot have parallels in the other great religions:

> . . . God's total self-communication in Jesus cannot simply be multiplied,
> for this would yield more than one absolute, and history as a whole,
> including the Parousia, would be split in two, whereas the one and only
> God has initiated a movement towards monotheism and his manifestation
> in Yahweh, a movement towards the gathering of all human beings under
> one God. This suggests all the more reason why he would wish to unite
> humanity through this unique and unsurpassable entry into history in
> Jesus Christ and not splinter humanity through other similar incarnations.
> . . . the Christ event is not simply a quantitative improvement in the
> religious development of humanity, not simply a blossom of surpassing
> beauty in the bountiful garden of religion, but an initiative and a revela-
> tion of God of absolute qualitative novelty, an unique event in salvation
> history. This is a claim we must continue to make throughout all the
> course of our efforts to reconcile the religions in unity (Buhlmann, p. 222).

At first sight Buhlmann's analysis seems to be a mere rehash of
the traditional Catholic position, but this is not so. He bases his
conclusions on an important distinction between an *exclusive* and
inclusive concept of salvation. For some three-hundred years after
the Reformation the Catholic Church developed a self-awareness as
an exclusive means to salvation ('outside the Church there is no
salvation'). Buhlmann claims that this misunderstanding originates
with a false interpretation of the Old Testament idea of Israel as the
'Chosen People' of God, a status which today is biblically understood not in an exclusive, sectarian way but as a model in which
God's salvific wish for *all* people becomes visible and tangible:

The choice of Israel is not to be understood exclusively. Israel's is the special case in which the election of all people is to become visible and tangible. Just as it was for the sake of the people that the Patriarchs and Prophets received their vocation, so Israel was called for the sake of the peoples, who are always on God's horizon (Buhlmann, p. 35).

From this renewed biblical understanding, Buhlmann argues that the Christian church cannot put itself forward as the exclusive beneficiary of salvation and revelation, but as a model of human fellowship wherein God's revelation to all peoples is made visible and tangible. Consequently, the Christian church, instead of guarding its own unique heritage or converting all other religions to its point of view, must become the main agent among all peoples for an awareness and ownership of the revelation God offers to all and makes more real and explicit in the Christian church. In this interpretation, the Christian church is given a special status regarding revelation, but not a position of power (as of old), but one of service to all other faiths, a service of ecumenical dialogue aimed at a conscientisation of all other faiths in an awareness of *their own* call to godliness.

All Christian writers, and Catholic ones in particular, feel deeply committed to the uniqueness and priority of Christian revelation. Readers familiar with Buhlmann's classic work, *The Coming of the Third Church,* cannot but admire his broadmindedness and his deep understanding of other faiths along with his sincere commitment to global, ecumenical dialogue. Clearly, he does not consider other faiths to be inferior to Christianity; the weakness of his presentation is in its failure to highlight the uniqueness of each individual faith and to use this as a starting point for a theology of religion.

Doing Theology Globally

Buhlmann's exposition indicates a significant shift in the Christian and Catholic understanding of revelation and of a genuine move towards a new global theology. It also reveals the tenacity and cautiousness with which Christian theologians are likely to move for some time to come. Increasingly one expects that a dialogue arising from the respective uniqueness of each religion, rather than from the traditional status of some over others, or from a felt obligation to give preference to one's own faith, will become the norm. Clearly, in this new vision, a readiness to enter in the spirit (and practice) of another religious perspective cannot, and must not, be considered a betrayal of one's own faith. Nor is it necessarily inappropriate to start from where we are, where the truth can be most real for each individual person. In fact, when we really touch the core truth of our own faith, then we enter the realm of that truth which has fascinated the heart and mind of man since primitive times and we are then in touch with the global, ecumenical spirit at the heart of all religion.

The emerging human and creative consciousness has a distinctive global, eclectic and non-dualistic flavour. Increasingly, we seem to be approaching an evolutionary stage of universal coherence. This new and gentle breeze enters our world from a diversity of vision and experience; to perceive and comprehend its impetus demands a new attitude and orientation from every field of contemporary science. Scholars, such as James Miller and Fritjof Capra, have already given us the framework for such an inter-disciplinary approach. No one branch of learning, sacred or mundane (irrelevant categories in the new holistic vision) can, on its own, comprehend or appreciate the evolutionary dynamism of our time.

The contemporary theologian cannot afford to miss this moment of grace. The changes taking place in today's world are profoundly spiritual and touch the inner core of both man and the universe. A new theology is in the making; if we choose to ignore it, it will happen without us, just as today, so much spiritual growth takes place outside rather than within the official churches.

Today's theologian must be, above all else, a person of *global vision*. Whether one starts from the experience of one's own personal faith or from a more ecumenical stance one must seek to foster a vision of universal holiness, a global pursuit for truth and transcendence. The theologian must confront the false gods of our age which divide the earth into the 'have's' and 'have-not's' and dismantle the outdated myths and ideologies which cripple human growth and creativity. The theologian must conscientise those encumbered by the shackles of legalism and institutionalism, creating an awareness of the one, universal God who cannot be contained within any system or structure. He must outgrow the petty prescriptions and quibblings which today absorb so much time and energy in theological deliberation. He must foster an air of tolerance and eclecticism to see the truth as diverse, pluriform and multifacited and not capable of being absorbed or expressed in any one religious system.

Secondly, today's theologian must be a person of *learning*, not in a narrow, academic sense but with the breadth and vision of mature, intellectual pursuit. The traditional Christian position, which considers Aristotelian/Thomistic philosophy to be the handmaid of theological reflection is no longer a viable paradigm. Today's theologian must be grounded in human experience – one's own and that of others – and be able to articulate for people the deep, transcendent aspirations of the human heart; familiarity with the social sciences, especially psychology, sociology and anthropology is essential for this pursuit. One must also be equipped to listen to the God of nature and, therefore, a knowledge of physics, biology and the natural sciences is desirable. History and folklore also embody something of the sacred – all history is sacred history and enriches the theologian's perception of reality. One is not suggesting the impossible – a thorough knowledge of everything, but an interdisciplinary, global, holistic and integrated understanding of life rather than the linear, over-ritualised, theological formation of earlier times.

Thirdly, the distinction between the *theologian* and the *mystic* has to become something of a misnomer. The contemporary dialogue between mysticism and physics poses a totally new challenge to our religious perception of reality. The mystical *rapport* of the person with creation – an old idea being revitalised – must also enter the theologian's experience of life if he hopes to cultivate in his life and work the global vision outlined above. The theologian's ability to decipher the voice and promptings of the Spirit through sacred text – Christian and otherwise – will continue to be an important part of theological reflection. And the emerging dialogue with all peoples and cultures will become the nucleus of the new hermeneutics.

Fourthly, theological *language* must, like theology itself, become the language of ordinary people and not just the official jargon of professionals, distanced from the people they are intended to serve. If theology in the past became insular and irrelevant to people, it was largely because of an exclusively inward-focused, academic thrust. The object of understanding and articulation tended to be the 'God-in-the-clouds', and not 'God-among-his-people'. A new theological language is not merely desirable for dialogue with believers but also, and in a special way, with atheists, whose purifying effect on the faith continues to be an important part of a religious culture.

Finally, tomorrow's theologian must be *prophetic*, not a mere 'yes' person, faithfully expounding and meticulously interpreting official doctrine, but challenging both believer and non-believer to deeper reflection, more authentic commitment and more creative praxis. The theologian's responsibility is primarily to people, not to systems or to institutions, no matter how sacred. It is also among the people and in their world that one will read the signs of God's action in the world and only in and with those same people can one make an authentic theological response. In this way, theology progresses from being a doctrine that can stifle to an action that renews and revitalises, a theology that lives, a theology that makes sense to people.

And by making sense to people, it will make sense of God. It will point to the God of all peoples, whose Spirit inhabits the heart of mankind individually and globally. It will articulate the human urge to posit this God in our own image and likeness, to make him accessible (initially), and it will alert us to our tendency to idolise this God in images which mar rather than enhance the true image. Finally, theology will seek to educate us to our own idolatrous perception wherby we create a God to fill our existential vacuum and then make him redundant when he becomes too real and challenging for us. The focus on God, which is concomitant with the perceptual search for meaning and happiness, is a human exploration, common to humankind in all ages and cultures. It is the theologian's task and privilege to enhance this exploration by liberating us from cultural conditioning and projecting us into the ever-new future of God's evolving revelation.

Bibliography

Buhlmann, Walbert, *The Coming of the Third Church*, Slough: St. Paul's, 1974

——, *The Chosen Peoples*, St. Paul's, 1982.

Capra, Fritjof, *The Tao of Physics*, Flamingo/Fontana, 1976.

——, *The Turning Point*, Flamingo/Fontana, 1982.

Davis, Charles, *Christ and the World Religions*, Hodder & Stoughton, 1970.

Dulles, Avery, *Models of Revelation*, Gill & Macmillan, 1984.

Knitter, Paul F., *No Other Name?: A Critical Survey of Christian Attitudes toward the World Religions*, SCM Press, 1985.

Mackey, James P., *The Problems of Religious Faith*, Chicago: Franciscan Herald Press, 1972.

Macquarrie, John, *Principles of Christian Theology*, SCM Press, 1966.

Miller, James, *Living Systems*, McGraw-Hill, 1978.

Nolan, Albert, *Jesus Before Christianity*, Darton, Longman and Todd, 1977.

Rahner, Karl, *Hearers of the Word*, Herder & Herder, 1969.

Thompson, William M., *Christ and Consciousness*, Paulist Press, 1977.

Tillich, Paul, *Systematic Theology*, Vol. 1, University of Chicago Press, 1957.

Smith, F. Harold, *The Elements of Comparative Theology*, Duckworth, 1937.

8

New Possibilities for Science and Religion
(Physics)

As far as the laws of mathematics refer to reality, they are not certain, and in so far as they are certain, they do not refer to reality. — ALBERT EINSTEIN

For the Western mind, this idea of the implicit unity of all opposites is extremely difficult to accept. — FRITJOF CAPRA

The most important function of science is to awaken the cosmic religious feeling and keep it alive. — ALBERT EINSTEIN

The universe begins to look more like a great thought than a great machine. — SIR JAMES JEANS

IN 1952 a strange event took place in the island of Koshima (southern Japan). Prior to that time a native monkey-species, *Macaca Fuscata*, used to come inland and forage for the sweet potatoes traditionally grown on the island. The monkeys ate the potatoes, grit and all, until 1952 when a young female monkey, whom the scientists have since named *Imo*, took the potatoes down to the sea and washed them before eating. Gradually other members of the family appropriated the new behaviour, until 1958 when it was discovered that every monkey in the colony had acquired the new skill, although the majority of the group had no contact whatever with *Imo* or her early associates.

Contemporary science has named this phenomenon *Morphic Resonance*. The theory states that when a certain percentage of a group reaches a new threshold of awareness, then that awareness informs the entire group, exerting on it a transforming influence. There is a variety of scientific opinion as to what the 'certain percentage' is: certainly no higher than 10%, and some venture to think that a threshold as low as 1% may be adequate to create the qualitative leap.

Philip Sheldrake ascribes three possible causes for this phenomenon: (a) the creative activity of an agency pervading and transcending nature; (b) a creative impulse immanent in nature; (c) blind or purposeless chance. Traditional science, with a passion for quantification and verification, is loath to enter this debate, considering such phenomena to be outside its reach; at best it will opt for the third explanation.

The Heritage of Albert Einstein

Ever since the introduction of Albert Einstein's *Theory of Relativity* in 1905, science cannot easily turn a blind eye to those developments which modify or alter the course of natural events. Relativity theory posits the need to accommodate all qualifying factors, whether subject to verification or not. The scientific horizon was even further expanded some twenty years later when Einstein, in collaboration with an international group of physicists, including Max Planck (Germany), Niels Bohr (Denmark), Louis de Broglie (France), Erwin Schrodinger (Austria), Werner Heisenberg (Germany) and Paul Dirac (Britain) formulated the *Quantum Theory* which states that how we probe matter affects its behaviour and form; that some particles exist so briefly that they are not real but 'virtual', and that well ordered reality – the whole of the universe – rests on chance and randomness at a sub-atomic level.

The one-time mechanistic view of the universe, the brain-child of Newtonian science and Cartesian philosophy, seemed no longer adequate as an explanation of physical reality. The traditional view, which aimed at an understanding of the individual parts and their respective ability to operate together for the good of the whole (machine) was considered not merely an inadequate explanation but also an inappropriate one. It would be some years yet before this conviction would be clearly articulated.

In 1927 Werner Heisenberg formulated the *Uncertainty Principle*, noting that in our descriptions of atomic phenomena there are pairs of concepts, or aspects, which are inter-related, and precision in the definition of one concept is only possible with a measure of uncertainty in the other. For a better understanding of this relation between pairs of concepts Niels Bohr introduced the notion of *complementarity,* to explain what he perceived to be a dual aspect of matter, sometimes in the form of particles, other times in the form of waves. Following this discovery, it was noted that at the subatomic level, matter does not exist with certainty at definite places, but rather shows 'tendencies to exist' along with tendencies 'to occur' (rather than actually occuring) at definite times and places. *Probability* rather than *certainty* became an accepted scientific category; furthermore, it was not merely probability of things but rather probability of interconnections (relationships). Finally, in 1928, Paul Dirac outlined his theory of *anti-matter,* claiming that all matter is created out of some imperceptible substratum, unimaginable and undetectible, but nonetheless, 'alive'. The breakthrough initiated by Einstein had come a long way.

The Expanded Paradigm

The seeds of the new scientific vision came to fruition in the 1960s. In 1963, Murray Gell-Mann at Caltech (California) and George Zweig at CERN (Geneva) independently accounted for a vast array of newly-discovered particles, consisting of smaller building blocks which they called *aces* (Zweig) and *quarks* (Gell-Mann), the name that has prevailed. Thus began the nailing of the quarks for which Gell-Mann received a Nobel physics award in 1969.

Meanwhile, John Bell, a physicist working in Switzerland, proposed in 1964 and mathematically confirmed in 1972, the mysterious connection between paired particles, even when they are long distances apart. According to *Bell's Theorem*, physical objects constitute an indivisible whole; if paired particles fly apart and the polarity of one is changed by an experimenter, the other changes instantaneously. The mysterious way in which they remain connected necessitates an explanation akin to that of the mystics' unitary vision.

Bell's discovery in 1972 was followed by yet another revolutionary breakthrough in 1977: the theory of *Dissipative Structures*, formulated by the Belgian physical chemist, Ilya Prigogine. This was the first major challenge to Sadi Carnot's *Second Law of*

Thermodynamics, which states that the amount of useful energy in a living system is continually being absorbed through heat, friction, etc., and thus the process of depleting energy will continue until the universe burns itself out.

Prigogine and his colleagues claim that the Second Law applies only in *closed* systems. If the process of depleting energy is taking place in an *open* system, energy and matter are taken in while entropy and end products are expelled. The incoming energy not merely replaces lost resources but replenishes the entire system with a new impetus for growth and expansion. According to Prigogine, this happens because living systems (e.g. the human body, the universe), are so designed that they act in a self-organising, self-regulating mode of action, capable of utilising to their own advantage the renewed energy generated by interaction with the environment. In open systems, therefore, the outcome is one of breakthrough rather than breakdown.

The survival-potential of living (open) systems (what Jantsch calls *autopoiesis*) undermines the most sacred dogmas of the classical scientific paradigm. Few today would blindly adhere to the mechanistic view of the universe, with all functions automated on the basis of cause and effect; mutual interdependence rather than 'cause and effect' is rapidly becoming the governing principle of universal life. The emerging paradigm views the universe as an *ecosystem*, maintained and sustained through a delicate balance of interconnecting forces (biochemical and others), acting in a self-regulatory, self-organising fashion, and somehow held together by the ozone layer in the upper atmosphere.

> In contrast to the mechanistic Cartesian view of the world the world view emerging from modern physics can be characterised by words like organic, holistic, ecological. . . The universe is no longer seen as a machine, made up of a multitude of objects, but has to be pictured as one indivisible, dynamic whole whose parts are essentially inter-related and can be understood only as patterns of a cosmic process. . .
>
> This is how modern physics reveals the basic oneness of the universe. It shows that we cannot decompose the world into independently existing smallest units. As we penetrate into matter, nature does not show us any isolated basic building blocks, but rather appears as a complicated web of relations between the various parts of an unified whole (Fritjof Capra, *The Turning Point*, pp. 66, 70).

This new scientific vision is extremely practical in its application to daily life. Not alone does it undermine our major perceptual assumptions (the way we perceive reality), but also our cultural/ historical norms arising from those perceptions. Both the science and religion of the twentieth century are deeply rooted in a fragmentary mind-set; we focus attention largely or exclusively on the parts of an object (be it the human body or the universe itself) and we assume that a correct understanding of each part (and its interaction with each other part) will yield a correct perception of the whole. In this rests many of our major problems, personal, social, national and international.

Contemporary medical practice in the west will serve as a crude but useful analogy. A person presenting with a headache will tend to be treated in terms of a malfunction in a certain part of the body, but in *holistic* medicine, the headache will be considered as a symptom of an illness affecting the entire or total personality and may be originally caused by factors extraneous to the person herself, e.g. environmental influences, problems in relationships, work pressures, consumption of alcohol or food allergies. In the first case the doctor is working out of a mechanistic model, in the second case, a holistic one. In the latter, we begin with the whole, not with the parts, and by setting aright the whole in its interaction with its environment, we create the conditions for the self-renewal of the individual parts. Thus, the new physics marks a radical departure from the manipulative and mechanisation of the technocrat and from the dichotomised theologies (body versus soul, material versus supernatural, God versus man, etc.) of western civilisation. It opens up new holistic, global possibilities in the light of which the Copernican revolution pales into insignificance.

Matter and Consciousness

So much for living matter! Inanimate matter, too, takes on a new meaning in the unfolding global vision. The British physicist, David Bohm, provides a new perspective for the integration of the animate and inanimate universe. According to Bohm, what we normally perceive in the world is the explicate or unfolded order of things, the manifest reality. But there is an underlying order that is father to this second-generation reality, namely, an unbroken wholeness, what he calls an *implicate, enfolded* order. To describe the implicate order, Bohm uses the analogy of the hologram, a three dimensional image, which, when illuminated at any point will show up the entire image. The whole is perceived to be enfolded in each part, thus forming a cosmic web of inter-relations, dynamic (as distinct from static) in nature and activated by a conscious life-force. Bohm has also coined the term *holomovement* to express this dynamic, *conscious* nature of reality, out of which all forms of the conscious universe flow.

To understand the implicate order, Bohm has found it necessary to regard consciousness as an innate and essential feature of universal life. He sees mind and matter as being interdependent and correlated but not causally connected. They are mutually unfolding projections of a higher reality which is neither matter nor consciousness. To enter this new realm of scientific enquiry an increasing number of scientists find themselves on the threshold of mysticism and those who take the leap find their scientific vision affirmed rather than undermined; at this level, physicists seem to be at a point of no return!

Could it be that contemporary science is articulating the traditional religious call to conversion and transformation in a language comprehensible to the people of our day? And what the Church once perceived as being a great enemy may become the prophetic voice inviting mankind to transcend its partial and fragmentary perceptions and embark on a journey of exploration into the underlying unity which grounds all created reality, animate and inanimate alike.

At the moment, Bohm's theory is at a tentative, experimental stage and earns credibility more from qualitative consistency than from quantitative verification. His thesis has been greatly enhanced by the work of the Stanford neurophychologist, Karl Pribram, who developed a holographic model of the brain in which visual perception is carried out through an analysis of frequency patterns, and visual memory is organised like a hologram. Consequently visual memory cannot be precisely localised within the brain since the whole is encoded in each part. The brain, therefore, has an innate propensity to receive information holographically, to perceive and interpret reality in its diversity and complexity in its multi-dimentional nature.

Pribram's discovery is not quite as original or revolutionary as it may initially seem. Already at the beginning of the century, psychologists, Max Wertheimer, Kurt Koffka and Wolfgang Kohler suggested that we perceive reality in *gestalts* (wholes), and individual objects or experiences make sense, not in isolation, but in the context of their environment. Our tendency towards linear thinking, towards simplicity at the price of simplification, may have little wisdom or justification, other than utilitarian and short-sighted expediency.

The expansion of scientific consciousness, and the profoundly spiritual vision on which it is projecting humanity, continues to unfold. The pursuit of nature's ultimate building blocks has continued with great impetus in CERN and in other such 'accelerators' over the past twenty years. In 1974, Burton Richter of Stanford came up with a fouth quark and in 1977, the fifth was discovered by Leon Lederman of Fermilab (near Chicago). Finally, in 1984, the final, long-sought-after sixth quark was discovered in CERN. The physicists named it 'top' or 'truth', because they had hoped that it was the moment of truth in which they could finally piece together the jigsaw of universal life.

It was a moment of truth, but not the quality of truth envisaged. Firstly came the strange discovery that the quarks functioned only in relationships of twos or threes (revealing, perhaps, a fundamental aspect of all created reality) and, secondly, their activity was predominantly that of wave-like patterns of energy, whose source and purpose now seemed more elusive than ever.

The discovery of the sixth quark has brought the physicists of the world to a paradoxically strange kind of precipice. Should they wait until they can create the conditions for particle collisions at higher energies in the hope of discovering the ellusive building blocks? (The British physicists say 'no' and have threatened to withdraw from CERN). Or should they take the 'dark leap of faith' into spirituality and mysticism, a pathway adopted by Fritjof Capra, Peter Russell, David Bohm, Brian Josephson, Erich Jantsch and others. For many this latter course is a painful betrayal of all they have held dear; for some it seems one way forward; for the few (Capra, etc.) it is the great breakthrough, the final truth of all scientific pursuit, the ultimate goal of scientific research, old and new.

Science and Religion: New Parameters

In the western world, science and religion have tended to go their respective ways, frequently ignoring each other and occasionally treating one another with scorn and suspicion. The Church's refusal to dialogue with Copernicus, Galileo, Pasteur, Darwin, to mention but a few, is already well documented and needs no further elaboration. Indeed, it serves as a classic example of the closed-system mind-set, with its accompanying bigotry and destructive divisiveness. At the end of the day, perhaps, the worst loser was the Church itself and, instead of preserving truth, only succeeded in alienating itself and many potential believers from the deeper, authentic truth which can only be reached through the diversity and universality inherent in open systems.

In one sense, the closed-mind debate goes on, with religion claiming to have a quality of access to ultimate answers which no other science can claim, and the physical sciences priding themselves in a methodology of quantification and verification which is assumed to produce a quality of certainty more real or authentic than that of any religious, mystical or esoteric system. Classical science simply does not want to know what religion has to say; it considers its academic purity to be best maintained within its own terms of reference, an orientation also adopted by traditional Christian belief systems. Meanwhile both systems (science and religion), consciously or unconsciously, have adopted an attitude of being the superior truth. But closed systems are ultimately doomed to extinction, as the Second Law of Thermodynamics has clearly elucidated. They burn themselves out, exhaust their potentialities in a high-energy absorbing task of isolated survival. The churches begin to lose their influence and membership declines, while science loses credibility even for its own practitioners. In the end, the proponents of these old models are likely to end up talking to nobody but themselves.

Of course, entrenchment rarely reaches such a critical stage. In a time of transition new fluctuations of energy (to use Prigogine's terms) move throughout a system. Up to a certain point we can dampen their effects and preserve what we consider to be 'structural integrity'. But when these fluctuations reach a critical size, they 'perturb' the system, they shake it up, create novel (perhaps unorthodox) interactions. The elements of the old pattern come into contact with each other in new ways and make new connections. The parts re-organise into a new whole. The system escapes into a higher order. The very instability created by innovation becomes the key to transformation. Open systems are not doomed to chaotic disorganisation; they inherit an innate propensity of life itself, to become life-giving and life-supporting, in a positive and powerful way.

Science and religion are embarking on a new dialogue but in a strange and unprecedented way. It is not a planned, organised dialogue between official representatives of both sides – the approach of the closed system. The impetus is coming from scientists who have been so gripped by a global vision of reality that they have instinctively coupled with believers of a similar orientation (mystics). In articulating this new dialogue both sides have transgressed not merely the traditional barriers between science and religion but worlds, considered so far apart, that they have never even been envisaged as barriers. The marriage of western science and eastern mysticism makes our western dogmatic mind-set (in both science and religion) seem trivial and even bizarre.

Explaining this new departure, Capra writes:

> We see that the ways of the modern physicist and the eastern mystic, which seem at first totally unrelated, have, in fact, much in common. It should not be too surprising, therefore, that there are striking parallels in their descriptions of the world. Once these parallels. . . are accepted, a number of questions will arise concerning their implications. Is modern science with all its sophisticated machinery, merely redicovering ancient wisdom, known to the Eastern sages for thousands of years? Should physicists, therefore, abandon the scientific method and begin to meditate? Or can there be a mutual influence between science and mysticism, perhaps, even a synthesis?
>
> I think all these questions have to be answered in the negative. I see science and mysticism as two complementary manifestations of the human mind; of its rational and intuitive faculties. The modern physicist experiences the world through an extreme specialisation of the rational mind; the mystic through an extreme specialisation of the intuitive mind. The two approaches are entirely different and involve far more than a certain view of the world. However, they are complementary. . . neither is comprehended in the other, but both of them are necessary, supplementing one another for a fuller understanding of the world. To paraphrase an old Chinese saying, mystics understand the roots of the Tao but not its branches; scientists understand its branches but not its roots. Science does not need mysticism and mysticism does not need science; but men and women need both. Mystical experience is necessary to understand the deepest nature of things, and science is essential for modern life. What we need, therefore, is not a synthesis but a dynamic interplay between mystical intuition and scientific analysis (*The Tao of Physics*, pp. 338-339).

With this breakthrough, the gods of both science and religion come tumbling down, and the God of all creation, of the Christian, the Buddhist, the Muslim and the Scientist, the God of all peoples, who for so long has been redundant, once more appears on our horizon. This is the God of our prehistoric ancestors, the one who forever transcends the categories, divisions and barriers of our limited vision, the God who is the mind of our universe (Jantsch), the catalyst at work in the heart of creation. Thanks to the physicists in particular, this God may once again be redeployed and lead her (his) people into the discovery of the new age that is dawning upon us.

Bibliography

Anon, 'How the Physicists Nailed the Quarks', *The Economist*, 5 January 1985, pp. 69-72.

Anon, 'Worlds Within the Atom', *The National Geographic*, 167 (May 1985), pp. 634-663

Capra, Fritjof, *The Tao of Physics*, Flamingo/Fontana, 1976.

——, *The Turning Point*, Flamingo/Fontana, 1982.

Cazenave, Michael (Ed.), *Science and Consciousness: Two Views of the Universe*, Pergamon Press,1984.

Ferguson, Marilyn, *The Aquarian Conspiracy*, Paladin, 1982.

Jantsch, Erich, *The Self-Organizing Universe*, Pergamon Press, 1980.

Kawai, M., 'Newly acquired precultural behaviour of the natural troop of Japanese monkies on Koshima Island', *Primates*, 6 (1965), pp. 1-30.

Russell, Peter, *The Awakening Earth*, Routledge and Kegan Paul, 1982.

Sheldrake, Phillip, *A New Science of Life*, Paladin Books, 1983.

Wilber, Ken (ed), *The Holographic Paradigm and other Paradoxes*, London: New Science Library, 1982.

9

Partners to a New Dialogue
(Atheism and Mysticism)

Mystics and schizophrenics find themselves in the same ocean, but the mystics swim whereas the schizophrenics drown.

— R.D. LAING

A rain of Gods descends from heaven on the funeral rites of the one unique God who outlived himself. Now atheists have their saints and blasphemers are building chapels.

— LESZEK KOLAKOWSKI

Non-religious man has lost the capacity to live religion consciously, and hence to understand and assume it; but in his deepest being he still retains a memory of it. — MIRCEA ELIADE

ATHEISM, in everyday usage, means the explicit negation of God and in practice this means living as if God did not exist. *Mysticism*, a feature of every world religion, with a diverse variety of expression, is described by Stevens in these words:

> Mysticism is the art of becoming fully conscious. It is the way of removing the filters. It is the path to getting fully in tune with reality. Mysticism is a new way of being that transforms everything it touches. It puts me in touch with my deepest self, my hidden powers. So profoundly does it transform me that the mystic state is described as touching the divine (pp. 15-16).

In practice, mysticism involves a process of inner purification, quite painful at times, which often results in abandoning the structures and obligations of formal religion, in order to reach a purity of divine truth itself. Atheism, too, denounces the God of the religious system, rather than the true God, who is frequently the implicit goal of the atheistic pursuit. In this way the mystical and atheistic paths follow parallel lines and quite frequently articulate a common desire for authenticity and truth.

A New Look at Atheism

In common usage, atheism has a negative and perjorative connotation. It depicts a state of complete denial of God's existence and the total irrelevance of the God concept for human life and meaning. But this description does not make sense, because man, being essentially a spiritual being, cannot endure without spiritual nourishment, just as the physical body needs food, air and rest in order to survive. Devoid of an inherited faith, spiritual beings create their own god or gods, that is, objects of transcendence, points of reference that elevate human existence onto a transcendental plane which gives meaning, purpose and direction to ordinary life, especially in its moments of heightened experience, positively or negatively. Our 'godless' being creates his own God; the very nature of his life and existence compels him to do so. His transcendence may find expression in very secular pursuits, even in self-destructive godliness (e.g. drugs, sex, money or power abuse), but he is worshipping 'gods' and his life is being directed by transcendent values, defying human rationale or explanation. Therefore, he cannot, in the strict sense, be described as atheistic.

Neither can we denote as atheistic the one who abandons the practice of formal religion, because that tends to happen for one of three reasons:

(a) The formal religion, because of its insipidity and lifelessness, no longer evokes genuine transcendent feelings or values for the devotee, a common feature of all comtemporary religious systems, highlighted in the weariness, apathy and boredom of today's alienated youth.

(b) The formal religion has lost its prophetic vitality and is no longer capable of challenging those forces which create oppression and human degradation, and consequently is failing to provide hope and a better future for the poor and oppressed. When the formal religion fails to be a prophetic leaven, people turn elsewhere, especially to a more practical 'faith', guaranteeing a better chance of a more hope-filled future (e.g. Marxism for many Third-world countries).

(c) Because it has outlived its usefulness, the formal religion is dying its natural death. In other words, atheism may be the name we give to the dying phase or death experience in the life-cycle of a formal religion; in using this name we may also be expressing the desirability (maybe even the necessity) of such dying. Not that the formal religion has become totally irrelevant; it may still serve massive numbers of its adherents, but in a manner that shields them from life, creating a false security, rather than challenging and inspiring people to a more transformative mode of existence. The formal religion has become a type of idolatry; the underlying myth no longer enables people to confront their world in a creative and compassionate way.

Formal atheism is a rare commodity. In the west the concept tends to be associated with the philosophical views of Nietzsche, Feuerbach, Freud, Russell, Marx and Sartre. However, the thoughts and ideas of these men are deeply religious and they write, not out of hatred for religion, but out of a deep, concerned love. They express in clear and vivid terms their own personal disillusionment and that of their contemporaries, with a religion that has become so ossified in churches and systems that it is no earthly or humanly good. If these philosophers go further and suggest the abolition of religion as, for example, Marx does, it is precisely because they perceive it as destructive to human life and dignity. Whatever we may say against the atheists of the eighteenth and nineteenth centuries, we cannot accuse them of being unconcerned; in fact, their writings provide expositions of *incarnational theology* (and profoundly prophetic, at times) which must be an embarrassment to many Christian theologians.

Péréz-Esclarín summarised the atheistic position of Nietzsche in these words:

> . . . humanistic atheism presents itself as the liberator of humanity and the champion of authentic humanism. . . it tends to emphasise faith in human beings rather than the denial of God. Thus, faith proposes to be a liberating praxis. As Camus once wrote: 'If the world has been and still is, inhuman with God, then we shall try to humanise it without God or against him.' Humanistic atheism rejects all deities who are antagonistic to humanity, all images of a being who prevents us from being fully human. . . God cannot be an impediment to authentic humanism. God can only be its supreme realisation (pp. 196, 197).

Committed atheists are delightful people to dialogue with and they tend to be happy to share their views and consider those of other persuasions. Their rejection of religion tends to be a form of protest, consciously or otherwise, against what they perceive to be pernicious or irresponsible attitudes, arising from adherence to formal religion. Thus, atheism becomes one of the most amenable and thoroughly purifying agents of religion.

Idolatry and Religious Indifference

There are pernicious forces at work in the contemporary spiritual world which we could beneficially address with some of the traditional warfare we wage with atheism. These are idolatry and indifference. Unlike atheism, they are subtle, subversive and camouflaged in a variety of forms. It is no harsh judgement to state that many people, who by traditional standards consider themselves to be very good adherents of one creed or another, are deeply idolatrous and have lost touch with the real God. One thinks of the massive numbers who faithfully attend religious services, devote much time and energy to devotional practices, but never lift a finger to help a neighbour in need or to rectify the social wrongs that create so much misery, pain and suffering in our society. One finds this form of idolatry in every major religion, adhered to not just by faithful devotees, but also propagated (consciously or otherwise) by churches, for status and financial gain.

A great deal of idolatry is subconscious, an infantile attachment to a specific myth, a fixated perception and understanding of life, which inhibits growth and progress and, in many cases, becomes a life-long dependency, even in pathological proportions; for example, one notes that in western countries at least, forms of mental illness with paranoia as a presenting symptom, tend to be preoccupied with a fear of God and his punishing power; such fear, which can be both intense and crippling (emotionally and spiritually), is the product of our infantile and unarticulated idolatry. Something of the ambivalence inherent in contemporary idolatry can be gleaned from these obervations of Péréz-Esclarín:

Since God is a hidden God, idolatry always remains our great temptation. Even believers will continue to be attracted to it because we need something tangible on which to pin our hopes. . . human beings have always tended towards idolatry whether they were religious or not. The tendency is so strong that they would invent a god if God did not exist. Even if God does exist, human beings are willing to kill him in order to justify their idolatry in the face of the ambiguities posed by life and their own behaviour (pp 60-61).

There are, however, other forms of idolatry, much more pervasive and culturally destructive. These include what Péréz-Esclarín calls 'the divinisation of science and the machine', 'the divinisation of sex' and 'the religion of consumption', what, elsewhere in this book, we call the gods of pleasure, power and prestige. These are the substitute or compensatory gods that accompany a great deal of religious *indifference* in today's world.

Such indifference is not a deliberate rejection of religion. People who drift away from formal religion, especially from religious practice, still claim they believe in God and wish to retain prayerful communication with God. Others just progressively drift away because formal religion does not seem to have any important bearing on their perception of life. Others, immersed in the materialism and functionalism of our technological society, become so robot-like in attitude and character that the spiritual dimension is never allowed to blossom; frequently such people are also aesthetically and emotionally impoverished. The entire intuitive, emotional and spiritual side of the personality has been suppressed and may remain so for an entire lifetime. A rebalancing, if it is to come about, will probably necessitate some powerful motivation, frequently arising from a crisis in the person's own life or in his immediate environment.

It has been suggested that religious indifference is a symptom of a mutation in consciousness (Willy Obrist), already referred to as the shift from the Newtonian-Cartesian, mechanistic paradigm to a more holistic, global, systems-based perception of reality. With the emerging and unfolding vision arises a move away from closely defined introspective and restrictive institutions to systems, more fluid and open and more receptive to the diversity and richness of life. The transition from the former to the latter takes place *via* the inevitable upheaval inherent in all transitions. Because of the enormity of this transformation which is cultural and global and definitely not religious in any traditional meaning of the term, the temptation towards (perhaps, the necessity for) trial and experiment is all the greater; therefore, we confront the breakdown in moral standards and traditional values and the emergence of cultural and behavioural patterns which can scarcely be described as life-giving.

Meanwhile, we have masses of people unconsciously drawn into the flow of change, drifting along with the emerging system, largely, if not totally unaware of what is happening. From this group we hear voices of disillusionment and a nostalgia for the past when everything was neat and simple and they knew exactly where they stood. Precisely because the official church no longer provides such security they may gradually abandon it, or maintain connection at a low level of commitment, ritually rather than for deep personal reasons; they may be too scared to abandon ship completely! Finally, those in the transition may become bitter and alienated and align themselves more on the side of atheism; from this vantage-point a new dialogue can begin, one that does not seem possible while people are caught in the indifferent, middle-of-the-road drift.

Both idolatry and indifference are rampant in today's society and are a dominant feature of the religious decline we experience in western culture. Emerging from the confusion and disillusionment are two prophetic strands which, initially, seem light years apart: atheism and mysticism. These are potentially the architects of a new religious design. We have referred briefly to the atheist as the purifier of religion. Let us now look at the emerging mysticism of contemporary spirituality.

The Mystical Vision

Mysticism, as the experience of God's unifying and encompassing power, is an aspect of all religions known to man. It has been, and continues to be, the dominating feature of the great eastern religions; hence, their strong individualistic flavour and their lack of a distinctive institutional or ecclesial structure. Christianity, on the other hand, being a structured religion from a very early stage and conscious of declaring its orthodoxy in the face of what it perceived to be heretical movements, has continually sought to accommodate mystical experience within its formal structures. Therefore, Clement of Alexandria and Origen considered mysticism to be the equivalent of the Pauline notion of *mystery*, with Jesus as the central focus. At a later stage it came to be identified with the sacraments, and like them was considered to be an outward sign of invisible grace (Dionysious the Areopagite). Subsequently, the term became synonymous with contemplation and to a lesser extent with asceticism and was reserved mainly to monks and virgins. This latter connotation continues to be its predominant focus of meaning.

The tendency in the Christian church to enclose mysticism within its formal teaching and structures betrays a certain fear of mysticism and the threat posed by its inherent challenging and purifying potential. The Gnostic heresy in the early church may be interpreted as a mystical movement (with its strong emphasis on direct knowledge of divinity without any human or church mediation) unable to flourish within the restrictive boundaries of the official church. Many so-called heretical movements in Christian history, e.g. the Cathari, Beghards and Beguines, Fraticelli and the Quietest movement of the seventeenth century all had a distinctive mystical orientation. The Christian church has never been at ease with its mystics and one is tempted to surmise that our great Christian mystics must have found the Christian church something of a contradiction. Neither is it a coincidence of history that some of the most outstanding Christian mystics, namely, Saints John of the Cross and Catherine of Sienna lived during what seems to have been one of the most powerful centuries of Christian mysticism while simultaneously the young Martin Luther was rapidly losing faith in what he perceived to be a depraved and corrupt church. Were the mystics and atheists perceiving the same reality and addressing the same basic problem from different angles?

According to Dionysious the Areopagite, the mystical experience, which defies human explanation, and cannot be induced by human techniques, consists of three stages: *purification, illumination* and *union*. The mystical life, therefore, is considered to be a foretaste of the recovery of paradise and a return to man's primeval unity prior to the fall, created by original sin.

The mystic is archetypal of man's ultimate, spiritual search. The mystical pursuit is one of pure truth and vision, an aspiration at the heart of both the person and the universe, a dream which seeks realisation at a primordial level of being. Mystical experience is described by William Johnston as a form of energy:

> . . . in mysticism, the very highest form of human energy is brought into play, a human energy that is nothing other than love at the core of one's being. . . Here a whole cosmic energy is unleashed and the world shakes (pp. 90-91).

The state of union to which the mystic is magnetically drawn is no mere 'other-worldly' union with a distant God. It is a sense of being at one with the godliness (i.e. the ultimate goodness) of all life, physical and spiritual alike. The fundamental yearning for such ultimacy throws the mystic into a state of inner turmoil in which false attachments to, and false perceptions of, life are purified (first stage), and the mystic experiences a sense of illumination (second stage), whereby intellectually, emotionally, humanly, one feels more at home in the world, absorbed in a new and profound perception of reality, what in contemporary psychology we may call a new *gestalt*.

The traditional idea of the mystic abandoning the world and frowning upon all that enhances the propogation of life is grossly misleading. *Mystics were not world-haters;* neither did they indulge in a spiritual fantasy of playing the perfection of God against the imperfections of man. They denounced corruption, greed, self-aggrandisement at the expense of others and they aspired towards a world of peace, love and justice, at harmony with its creator and consciously proceeding towards the unfolding of its ultimate destiny. In the mystics, claims Johnston, the world experiences purification and healing and, hence, creation is set free to evolve with greater energy and purpose. In this way, we may suggest that the mystic becomes the *passive* agent of spiritual growth, while the atheist becomes its *active* agent. One is not suggesting that one is more powerful than the other; they simply represent two poles between which the vital energies of all growth continually fluctuate.

Mysticism: East and West

At this point, the western mystical vision can link up with that of the east. Chinese philosophy (which does not distinguish the material from the spiritual) has always considered the *Tao* (a life-giving process of continual flow and change) to be the core of all reality. All created objects, animate and inanimate, have their Tao or 'heart' which gives them meaning and uniqueness. The principal characteristic of the Tao is the cyclic nature of its ceaseless motion, the continual fluctuation between what the Chinese call the *Yin* and the *Yang*, the archetypal poles indicating the unbroken interplay of opposites for the good of the whole. It is not therefore their *opposite-ness* that is important but rather the dynamic, creative interaction which is not possible without the opposites. Contrary, therefore, to traditional Greek dualism, with its profound influence on the Christian and western value-systems, the east, and the Chinese in particular, have inherited a distinctively holistic way of perceiving life, one that has profoundly influenced their attitude and approach to living reality, religion included.

According to the Chinese I Ching, the Yang having reached its climax retreats in favour of the Yin; the Yin having reached its climax retreats in favour of the Yang. Yin is associated with the feminine, the earth, moon, night, winter, moisture and interiority; the Yang with the masculine, heaven, sun, day, summer, dryness and surface. In relation to people, the Chinese believe that everybody, male and female, goes through Yin and Yang phases. Culturally, life is at its optimum when the Yin-Yang interaction is well balanced, although this balance will never be in a full state of equilibrium.

The emerging dialogue with the east has greatly enhanced our western understanding of mysticism and has helped to salvage the concept from the esoteric, super-human and other-worldly sphere in which it could decompose for time immemorial. The dialogue with the east has broadened our horizons even further to accommodate the insights of psychology and other scientific disciplines relating to psychic states. Arising from this creative interplay of diverse disciplines and diverse cultural strands we begin to feel and behold the ultimate mystery which gives meaning, coherence and purpose to all living things. Once we feel this sense of mystery and allow ourselves to be touched by its magic, then we begin to enter the mystical experience; we begin to touch our deepest origins; we begin to see the web of interconnections: with each other, with the earth we inhabit and the God who continually invites us to participate in the mysterious unfolding of life. Mystical experience is not intended to be the reserve of the few; the great mystics of history are merely symbolic of a fundamental birthright we all possess, namely the ability to perceive life in its dynamic, creative totality and to respond accordingly.

The mystical response is both a Yin and a Yang. It is a holistic response, not one dissected by superficial distinctions of Greek dualism, nor by a distorted religious view necessitating the many false gods who either imprison us in a self-consuming fire of infantile devotion or in an agitated and dissipated absorption by the deities of power, pleasure and prestige. The mystical response is a life-giving one, open to the mystery of life at every level of existence, even at levels as yet unrevealed by the course of evolution. There are no limits to mystical perception, just as there are no known limits to the mystery of life.

Agents of Purification

We have already described the relationship between atheism and mysticism as one of opposite but complementary energies, the passive and active, with neither being necessarily more powerful than the other. Although a useful model, it has a number of serious limitations. Both mysticism and atheism can be passive and/or active. We tend to associate mysticism with the solitude of the desert and the mortification of the hermit; we tend to associate atheism with negative protest and denunciation. Both associations are the product of a particular cultural and religious paradigm, based more on a dualistic rather than a holistic view of life. Both movements seek purification of cultural and religious motivation and aspire towards a more enlightened understanding of the divine-human relationship. Atheism may superficially betray a strong dislike of, and even disrespect for, official religion, an attitude not infrequently caused by the intransigent stance often adopted by churches throughout the course of history. One is not suggesting that the positive qualities of atheism are on par with·those of mysticism (which can also be misguided and dangerously close to perversion, at times). All one wishes to assert is that both movements seek in diverse ways, the 'heart' of true religion.

In the emerging world-view of the late twentieth century, with the breakdown of traditional dichotomies, the contemporary religious dialogue becomes progressively global. We detect the first signs in an east-west dialogue and an awakening interest in the faith of our primitive ancestors. The dialogue is incomplete without listening, too, to those subtle and powerfully corrective and purifying agents of our faith: atheists and mystics. Without their presence, we cannot hope to reach the truth that sets us free.

Bibliography

Capra, Fritjof, *The Tao of Physics*, Flamingo/Fontana, 1976.

Greeley, Andrew, *Religion: A Secular Theory,* New York: Free Press, 1982.

Happold, F.C. *Religious Faith and Twentieth Century Man*, Pelican, 1966.

Johnston, William, *Silent Music*, Collins, 1977.

Obrist, Willy, 'Indifference to Religion: Symptom of a Mutation of Consciousness', *Concilium*, May, 1983, pp. 41-48.

Péréz-Esclarín, Antonio, *Atheism and Liberation*, SCM Press, 1980.

Six, Jean François, *Is God Endangered by Believers?* Dimension Books, 1983.

Stace, Walter, *The Teaching of the Mystics*, New American Library, 1960.

Stevens, Edward, *An Introduction to Oriental Mysticism*, Paulist Press, 1973.

10

Homo Novus:
A New Religious Horizon

Christian themes are ferments, not relics. — RAY L. HART

Revelatory experiences disclose to us that in the final analysis our relationship to mystery is gracious. — JOHN SHEA

Not only is there a new man on the horizon, but he brings with him a new world. — TOM HANNA

The Church is missing its chance to arrive in the world of tomorrow. — WALBERT BUHLMANN

AS A CHILD, I remember standing at the verge of the sea and I felt the sands moving beneath my feet. I fell, but because I was in shallow water, nothing much happened. Had I been in deep water, being unable to swim, I would probably have drowned. Somewhere deep in my subconscious my fear of the shifting sands still remains. Now that I can swim that fear does not control my life any more. Had I never learned to swim my fear of the sea would have denied me many hours of joy and relaxation.

And yet, what is wrong with shifting sands? Perhaps it is part of the grand plan that they should shift! Is the shifting of the sands not part of the great tidal heart-beat, the universal pulsation of life? There is something about the sea that puts one in touch with the rhythm of life itself: 'his strong heart stirs the ever beating sea' (Joseph Mary Plunkett). Those waves roll on ceaselessly, the tides rise and fall, the sands move and yet always remain. So why fear the shifting sands?

Where does the fear come from? — certainly not from the sands.

We are, in fact, the creators of our own fears, some of which cripple us for an entire lifetime. And it is not the intention of the shifting sands to spoil our fun or ensnare us in difficulty – this will only arise from our own limitations. Therefore, to be at ease with the shifting sands we need special resources, namely the ability to swim; with this asset our perception of the shifting sands changes completely.

Dialogue is Liberating

Writing the present book has been for me very much an experience of the shifting sands. So many cherished beliefs, couched in the dogmatic firmness of the church which once claimed (and still subtly does) that outside its own ranks there is no salvation, seem to be shifting beneath the feet. It has not been a comfortable experience.

Yet, there has been something tremendously liberating in being able to dialogue with other religious perspectives, especially those which predate all forms of official religion. I would like to suggest that this *global vision*, encompassing the hopes, fears, dreams and aspirations of all mankind, from the beginning until now, including the future we are evolving towards, is the equivalent of the swimming ability in coping with the shifting sands.

I expect that many who read this book have been culturally conditioned through home, school or society to perceive religious systems as being very different from each other. Consequently, a Catholic may consider himself to have a different understanding of faith from his Protestant neighbour and more than a different understanding, in fact, a completely different religion, from his Hindu or Buddhist friend. And there *are* differences, some of which are real (in terms of our perception) but most of which are contrived and fossilised over time.

At the core or heart of all religion is a human yearning for a fulfilment and happiness which humanity, while on this earth, is not capable of achieving, individually or communally. In the first chapter, therefore, we postulate that religion is a human creation or invention. Prior to the evolution of man, religion did not exist and its creation as an aspect of human life took place over some 70,000 years down to our own day.

Religion Comes From Within

The human need for religion, as explained in chapters 2 and 3 is first and foremost internal. It arises from a deep inner place, within each individual person, unlocated and not necessarily confined to the physical body, and in some mysterious way connected, too, to a corresponding 'heart' in the universe itself. What proof have we for all this? None, in terms of modern secular science which, in the northern hemisphere, at least, is considered to be the most thoroughly objective form of scrutiny available to contemporary man. Religion, however, unlike other aspects of human life, is subject neither to proof nor disproof.

Religion is not a neat conceptual package which can be subjected to analysis. Religion is a dimension of *experience,* universal experience, located within humanity, individually and globally; it can only be experienced at its own authentic core. Any effort to transmit that experience is incomplete, at least at this point in our evolution as human beings. We can talk about the experience, observe it, analyse it, re-enact it in a vast range of religous rite and ceremony, but since each person's experience is unique and only partial in terms of the global experience (Jung's collective unconscious) our observation will remain incomplete. Mystics of every religious tradition speak extensively of the non-communicable nature of religious experience.

The religious aspiration is, therefore, primarily internal (that is not to say *private*) and that inner capacity for religion we call the *spiritual* dimension, which we consider to belong to the entire human species. It unfolds uniquely in each person and is expressed in a variety of social and cultural ways. The 'why' and 'whence' of this spiritual domain we cannot determine with certitude or precision. Our vagueness about the spiritual is no different from that of many other dimensions of human behaviour, especially at the psychic and aesthetic levels of being.

It has been suggested that all our behaviour is geared towards and conditioned by our survival instinct, in the purely biological sense. The human capacity for play, art, music, literature, intellectual pursuit and sexual intimacy is far more fundamental than any urge to survive.

This deeper layer of human experience belongs to the spiritual urge, which may in fact be the deepest layer of all, that is, the most powerful and integrative force in human life. Whether we consider this inner core to be a direct creation of God or just a mysterious dimension of our nature, matters little. Once we acknowledge and accept it we can scarcely escape the conclusion that it connects us definitively and permanently with the source of life itself, whether we call that source 'God', or by some other name.

Spirituality comes from within – from within man as an individual and as a species. And its target of reference is life without: social life, physical life, all aspects of life, connecting human beings to their environment. To express this inner orientation in its inter-action with the human environment, our ancestors created religious rituals, rites and ceremonies from which eventually emerged the major religious systems known in our world today.

Religion as a Meaning-System

Let us now look at the external expression in greater detail. Religion, as indicated earlier, is largely concerned with meaning, a mode of reflection articulated in symbolic action and interaction, arising from a need to make sense of one's life and feel at home in one's world. In this process we transcend (not escape) the ambiguities and ambivalences of life and project hope and meaning into our existence. We do this at many levels, not just the religious one, since our spiritual nature informs all aspects of the human personality.

The spiritual aspiration for ultimate meaning can become energised in a variety of passionate concerns, especially where human feelings run deep and strong, e.g. sexuality, power, prestige; and, therefore, sex, money, power, glory can become 'gods' in our lives. In fact, these secular gods can dominate our lives and determine our values while, nominally we still claim to worship the God of formal religion, maybe out of routine or for social acceptability. In this case, both the secular and religious gods are mere fabrications, and idolatry rather than genuine religion has become the *raison d'être* of our existence.

As a meaning-system within society, religion has a power for cohesion and human brotherhood. When religion is authentically lived, it becomes a strong motivating force for the creation of a society marked by justice, compassion and love. It is often said, and indeed with good reason, that European Christianity reinforces the capitalistic value-system and this, undoubtedly, is a departure from the true nature of religion. On the other hand, the quality of

Christian faith emerging in Third World countries, especially in the Latin American subcontinent, gives the social dimension of the Gospel very concrete and challenging expression. The social component of religious belief seems to be particularly open to abuse and misinterpretation. The 'brotherhood of believers' tends, over time, to take on an ideological stamp in which religious law and practice tends to become the norm guaranteeing fidelity and conformity. This position of entrenchment points to corruption, decay and impending decline of that particular system.

Another pointer to fragmentation is the polarisation of the *social* and the *spiritual*, reminiscent of the Church versus State division. In this case, religion is considered to be about private faith and morality which is portrayed as a 'better state', above and beyond the concerns of secular society in which religious man should not become too immersed. This mentality, which one frequently encounters in some Christian groups, tends to view religion as a divine gift bestowed only on the selected few of God's special choice, not to be tarnished or defaced by the falseness of secularity which cannot accept its mysterious content.

This superior attitude leads us to consider one of the major tenets of established religion, namely, *revelation*. Most of the major religions lay their claim to authenticity on an explicit, definitive self-disclosure of 'God', by which divinity entered the world, laying claim to human submission and allegiance. According to the Christian faith, God intervened in the Old Testament (pre-Christian) times through his chosen ambassadors, Abraham, Moses, Jeremiah, etc. Then, 'when the fullness of time had come', God intervened directly in the human form of Jesus of Nazareth, disclosing through Jesus and through the church which claims to be the only authentic interpreter of the Jesus event, the divine plan for the world (as understood in the Christian context). Christianity, like the other world religions has, always considered itself to be the only true religion, a position somewhat changed in recent decades as we noted in chapter 7.

The question of revelation and its unique form in each religious system will continue to be a subject of debate for quite a long time, simply because it has been so much ignored in the past. It seems to be one of those delicate issues we can only dialogue about as we approach a new depth of evolutionary awareness. Man's religious consciousness as it has emerged over some 70,000-80,000 years is too diverse and complex to be synthesised in any set of religious systems deemed to be permanently necessary for man's spiritual development. Religion will always need a climate of openness, diversity and flexibility if it is to respond to the variety of human needs emerging at each new stage of evolution.

That is not to say that religious systems are irrelevant – far from it! As social beings we need structures to embody, and vehicles to express, the myths which give meaning to our existence. The rhythm and flow of our lives also demands a creative permanence, one we retain while it serves our best needs, one we can easily discard when it threatens to distort and blur our vision. Apparently, the human heart has not yet attained that wisdom whereby we can reach the happy medium between the stability that nourishes and the permanence that destroys.

Unity of Vision – Diversity of Expression

The second major area of tension is between diversity and conformity. I do not envisage one, universal religion, nor am I implicitly saying that all religions are the same; this is clearly not the case. All religions are human efforts to communicate with the ultimate source of life. Whether we consider this ultimate reality one or many, personal or impersonal, distant or near, very much depends on how the basic myth of each religious system articulates its effort at reconciling these opposites.

The ultimate synthesis will never satisfy all adherents. If it did, it would have lost touch with the great universal mystery transcending all individual aspirations and would be merely a human fabrication, capable of commanding neither respect nor allegiance. Moreover, to command credibility, each individual culture, or subculture, must create a religious system resonating with its own unique myth and symbolic forms. Any attempt to impose a religion of one culture on the people of another dominant culture seems to offend and contradict all the principles of cultural evolution. And this, of course, raises more awkward questions for religions such as Christianity with a strong missionary orientation.

Each major religion presumably arose from a dominant myth of a specific cultural origin and was created as a response to specific mythical and cultural needs. Whether or not it serves those needs today is a highly disputable question. In many cases it obviously does not, because the fundamental myth, even the culture itself has changed; the course of evolution makes such change inevitable. The fact that major religious systems fail to change to meet new needs (and consequently stagnate and die – perhaps over a few hundred or a few thousand years) indicates that the one-time myth has become an ideology and the original religion has effectively become a form of idolatry.

The ability to recognise our false idols, the humility to acknowledge their existence and the courage to declare them defunct and work towards their abolition from our shallow and corrupt value-systems, is the purifying service rendered by atheism in every age (cf. chapter 9). For the real atheist, God is not dead – he has simply been made redundant and replaced by false idols whom the atheist does not like. Long live the atheists – they are prophets in disguise.

Religion and the Future of Civilisation

Just as the shifting sands are an integral part of the seashore, so too is the variety of religious experience and expression integral to the growth of a healthy civilisation. Even atheism has its cherished place. Modern pluralistic society tends to accommodate this diversity. The churches, however, are still quite intransigent; they speak endlessly about ecumenical endeavours, while theologians babble ceaselessly about the God of all peoples, but attitudes change slowly. Meanwhile the masses of uncommitted, not the atheists (who are sufficiently committed to state their opposition, usually for serious even if misguided reasons), the apathetic and indifferent increase and multiply. Among the indifferent are many non-swimmers, swept off their feet by the shifting sands, disillusioned because the security of yesterday's church is no longer here; bored by the preponderous repetition of empty formulae, searching for an anchor of meaning which gets lost in the out-dated language and ritual of contemporary religion, or yet, shocked and disgusted when changes take place. And as they dig their heels in, the sands only shift further from beneath their feet.

And it is not in the religious sphere alone that our indifferent 'non-swimmers' get into trouble. The breakdown of their religious meaning-systems culminates in either a panic to grasp onto anything that offers safety and security, and hence, the secular idols of sex, money, drugs, power, etc., or they drown tragically in an attitude of disillusionment, alienation and despair, a trend which increasingly, in our society, is terminated in suicide.

Sociologists and historians rightly point to the crippling effect wrong religious attitudes have had on progress and civilisation; but this is only part of the picture. Religion, more than any other human phenomenon, has shaped the fortune and growth of our universe, especially in prehistoric times. Religion still remains a powerful catalyst for growth, progress and change. It all depends on how we human beings use it; it is one of life's greatest gifts to us; its wisdom and destiny is in our hands:

> Man judges rightly that by his intellect he surpasses the material universe, for he shares in the light of the divine mind . . . The intellectual nature of the human person is perfected by wisdom and needs to be. For wisdom gently attracts the mind of man to a quest and a love for what is true and good. Steeped in wisdom man passes through visible realities to those which are unseen.
>
> Our era needs such wisdom more than bygone ages if the discoveries made by man are to be further humanised. For the future of the world stands in peril unless wiser men are forthcoming (Pastoral Constitution on the Church in the Modern World, 212-213).

Out of the ashes and pains of a dying, mechanistic world-view and a declining western civilisation, our redundant God has new opportunities for employment in the emerging global consciousness, in the creative perception of reality, in the new holistic paradigm, in the evolutionary zest for life, in the birth of *Homo Novus*. As the swimmers survive in the shifting sands, so hopefully, the new wisdom which this book seeks to impart, will enhance our capacity for belief in the new age that is dawning upon us.

Bibliography

Abbott, Walter, M. (Ed.), 'Pastoral Constitution on the Church in the Modern World' in *The Documents of Vatican II*, Chapman, 1967, pp. 199-308.

Cohen-Richards, Fred & Anne, *Homo Novus: The New Man*, Colorado: Shields Publishing Inc., 1973.

Greeley, Andrew, *The Persistence of Religion*, SCM Press, 1973.

Leech, Kenneth, *The Social God*, Sheldon Press, 1981.

Sorokin Pitrim A., *Modern Historical and Social Philosophies*, New York: Dover Publications, 1950.

Select Bibliography

Abbott, Walter M., *The Documents of Vatican II*, Chapman, 1967.

Allport, Gordon, *Man and His Religion*, Macmillan, 1950.

Beals, R. L. and Hoijer, H., *An Introduction to Anthropology*, Collier-Macmillan, 1965.

Bellah Robert, *Beyond Belief*, London: Harper & Row, 1970.

Bennet, J. G., *The Dramatic Universe*, Hodder & Stoughton, 1966.

Berger, Peter, *A Rumour of Angels: Modern Society and the Rediscovery of the Supernatural*, London: Allen Lane, 1970.

——, *The Sacred Canopy: The Social Reality of Religion*, Harmondsworth: Penguin, 1973.

——, *The Heretical Imperative: Contemporary Possibilities of Religious Affirmation*, Collins, 1980.

Bergounioux, F. M. & Goetz, J., *Prehistoric and Primitive Religions*, London: Burns & Oates, 1965.

Boros, Ladislaus, *Meeting God in Man*, Burns & Oates, 1968.

——, *Hidden God*, Search Press, 1973.

Buhlmann, Walbert, *The Coming of the Third Church*, St. Paul's, 1974.

——, *The Chosen Peoples*, St. Paul's, 1982.

Campbell, Joseph, *The Masks of God: Primitive Mythology*, The Viking Press, 1959.

Capra, Fritjof, *The Tao of Physics*, Flamingo/Fontana, 1976.

——, *The Turning Point*, Flamingo/Fontana, 1982.

Clarke, R. & Hindley, G., *The Challenge of the Primitives*, London: Cape, 1975.

Collins, Desmond, *The Human Revolution: From Ape to Artist*, Oxford: Phaidon, 1976.

de Chardin, Teilhard, *The Phenomenon of Man*, Collins/Fontana, 1959.

——, *The Divine Milieu*, Collins/Fontana, 1960.

——, *The Hymn of the Universe*, Collins/Fontana, 1961.

——, *The Future of Man*, Collins/Fontana, 1964.

de Waal Mulefijt, Annemarie, *Religion and Culture*, Collier-Macmillan, 1968.

Dubos, Rene, *The God Within: A Positive View of Mankind's Future*, Abacus Books, 1976.

Eliade, Mircea, *The Sacred and the Profane*, New York: Torch Books, 1961.

——, *Shamanism: Archaic Techniques of Ecstasy*, Pantheon Books, 1964.

——, *The Quest: History and Meaning in Religion*, University of Chicago Press, 1969.

——, *Rites and Symbols of Initiation: The Mysteries of Birth and Rebirth*, London: Harvill Press, 1961.

——, *A History of Religious Ideas*: Vol. 1: *From the Stone Age to the Eleusinian Mysteries*, University of Chicago press, 1978.

Fallding, Harold, *The Sociology of Religion*, McGraw-Hill, 1974.

Farb, Peter, *Humankind*, London: Cape, 1978.

Fordham, Frieda, *An Introduction to Jung's Psychology*, Penguin, 1953.

Fowler, James W., *Stages of Faith*, Harper and Row, 1981.

Frankl, Victor, *Man's Search for Meaning*, Clarion books, 1959.

Frazer, J.G. *The Golden Bough: A Study in Magic and Religion*, Macmillan & Co., 1967 (abridged edition).

Fromm, Erich, *The Sane Society*, New York: Fawcett World Library, 1967.

——, *The Heart of Man: Its Genius for Good and Evil*, Harper & Row, 1980.

Greeley, Andrew, *The Persistence of Religion*, SCM Press, 1973.

——, *Religion: A Secular Theory*, New York, Free Press, 1982.

Gribben, John, *Genesis*, London: Dent, 1981.

Griffiths, Bede, *Return to the Centre*, Collins, 1976.

Happold, F.C., *Religious Faith and Twentieth Century Man*, Pelican, 1966.

Hockett, C. F., *Man's Place in Nature*, McGraw-Hill, 1973.

Hoebel, E. A. & Weaver, T., *Anthropology and the Human Experience*, McGraw-Hill, 1979.

Huizinga, Johan, *Homo Ludens: A Study of the Play Element in Culture*, Beacon Press, 1950.

Huxley, Julian, *The Humanist Frame*, Allen & Unwin, 1961.

James E. O., *Comparative Religion*, Methuen, 1961.

Jantsch, Erich, *The Self-Organizing Universe*, Pergamon Press, 1980.

Johnston, William, *Silent Music*, Collins/Fount paperback, 1977.

Jung, Carl, *The Collected Works of Carl Jung* (editors: Gerhard Adler, Michael Fordham and Herbert Read), Routledge & Kegan Paul;

——, Vol. 11: *Psychology and Religion: West and East* (1958)

——, Vol.12: *Psychology and Alchemy* (1944)

Koppers, Wilhelm, *Primitive Man and his World Picture*, Sheed & Ward, 1952.

Kubler-Ross, Elizabeth, *On Death and Dying*, The Macmillan Co., 1969.

Lacroix, Jean, *The Meaning of Modern Atheism*, Dublin: Gill, 1965.

Leakey, Richard E., *The Making of Mankind*, New York: E. P. Dutton, 1981.

Leslie, Paul, *Alternatives to Christian Belief*, Doubleday, 1967.

Ling, Trevor, *A History of Religion East and West*, The Macmillan Press, 1979.

Lissner, Ivar, *Man, God and Magic*, London: Cape, 1958.

Lovelock, James, *Gaia: A New Look at Life on Earth*, Oxford University Press, 1979.

Luckmann, Thomas (in association with Peter Berger), *The Social Construction of Reality*, Penguin, 1979.

Malinowski, Bronislaw, *Myth in Primitive Psychology*, Connecticut: Negro University Press, 1971.

Mannheim, Karl, *Ideology and Utopia*, Routledge and Kegan Paul, 1960.

Metz, J., *Theology of the World*, Search Press, 1969.

Miller, James, *Living Systems*, McGraw-Hill, 1978.

Moltmann, J., *Theology of Hope*, SCM Press, 1967.

McKern, Sharon and Thomas, *Tracking Fossil Man: An Adventure in Evolution*, London: Wayland, 1972.

Mackey, James P., *The Problems of Religious Faith*, Chicago: Franciscan Herald Press, 1972.

Macquarrie, John, *Principles of Christian Theology*, SCM Press, 1966.

O'Dea, Thomas F., *The Sociology of Religion*, Prentice-Hall, 1966,

Oesterley, William O.E., *The Sacred Dance*, Cambridge University Press, 1923.

Otto, Rudolf, *The Idea of the Holy*, Oxford University Press, 1958.

Padovano, Anthony, *The Estranged God: Modern Man's Search for Belief*, Sheed & Ward, 1966,

Péréz-Esclarín, Antonio, *Atheism and Liberation*, SCM Press, 1980.

Radin, Paul, *Primitive Religion: Its Nature and Origin*, London: Hamish Hamilton, 1938.

Riesmann, David, *The Lonely Crown*, New Haven: Yale University Press, 1961.

Robinson, John A. T., *Exploration into God*, SCM Press, 1967.

Russell, Peter, *The Awakening Earth: Our Next Evolutionary Leap*, Routledge & Kegan Paul, 1982.

Schmidt, Roger, *Exploring Religion*, California: Wadsworth Inc., 1980.

Shea, John, *Stories of God*, Chicago: The Thomas More Press, 1978.

———, *Stories of Faith*, Chicago: The Thomas More Press, 1980.

Smart, Ninian, *The Religious Experience of Mankind*, Collins/Fount paperback, 1969.

———, *The Concept of Worship*, Macmillan Press, 1972.

Smith, F. Harold, *The Elements of Comparative Theology*, Duckworth, 1937.

Sorokin, Pitrim, *Modern Historical and Social Philosophies*, New York: Dover Publications, 1950.

Stace, Walter, *The Teachings of the Mystics*, New York: New American Library, 1960.

Stevens, Edward, *An Introduction to Oriental Mysticism*, Paulist Press, 1973.

Suzuki, D. T., *Mysticism: Christian and Buddhist*, Collier Books, 1962.

Turner, Victor, *The Ritual Process: Structure and Anti-Structure*, Chicago: Aldine, 1968.

Wach, Joachim, *The Sociology of Religion*, University of Chicago Press, 1944.

———, *Types of Religious Experience, Christian and Non-Christian*, Routledge and Kegan Paul, 1951.

———, *The Comparative Study of Religions*, Columbia University Press, 1958.

Washburn, S. L. (Ed.), *Social Life of Early Man*, Methuen, 1962.

Watson, Lyall, *Supernature*, Hodder & Stoughton, 1973.

———, *Lifetide*, Hodder & Stoughton, 1979.

Wosien, Maria-Gabriele, *Sacred Dance: Encounter with the Gods*, London: Thames & Hudson, 1974.

Index